By Archibald MacLeish

Poems

Collected Poems, 1917–1952
including Conquistador, Streets in the
Moon, New Found Land, Actfive, The
Trojan Horse, and others

Songs for Eve

Plays in Verse

Panic
The Fall of the City
Air Raid
This Music Crept by Me upon the
Waters
J.B.

J.B.

a play in verse

HOUGHTON MIFFLIN COMPANY BOSTON
THE RIVERSIDE PRESS CAMBRIDGE
1958

J.B.

BY ARCHIBALD MacLEISH

TITLE PAGE AND END PAPER
DESIGNS BY ISMAR DAVID

The Prologue of *J.B.* first appeared, in somewhat different
form, in the September 1, 1956, issue of *The Saturday Review*.

Library of Congress Catalog Card Number: 57–10788
First Printing

𝕿𝖍𝖊 𝕽𝖎𝖛𝖊𝖗𝖘𝖎𝖉𝖊 𝕻𝖗𝖊𝖘𝖘
Cambridge, Massachusetts
Printed in the U.S.A.

J.B.

The scene throughout is a corner inside an enormous circus tent where a side show of some kind has been set up. There is a rough stage across the corner, on the left of which a wooden platform has been built at a height of six or seven feet. A wooden ladder leans against it. To the right is a deal table with seven straight chairs. There is a door-shaped opening in the canvas to the right rear. Above, a huge, slanted pole thrusts the canvas out and up to make the peak of the corner. Clothes that have the look of vestments of many churches and times have been left about at one side and the other of the stage and the light at the beginning — such light as there is — is provided by bulbs dangling from hanks of wire. The feel is of a public place at late night, the audience gone, no one about but maybe a stage-hand somewhere cleaning up, fooling with the lights.

THE PROLOGUE

Mr. Zuss, followed by Nickles, enters from the dimness off to the left. They stop at the edge of the side-show stage. Both wear the white caps and jackets of circus vendors. Both are old. Mr. Zuss, who has a bunch of balloons hitched to his belt, is large, florid, deep-voiced, dignified, imposing. Nickles is gaunt and sardonic; he has a popcorn tray slung from straps across his shoulders. Both betray in carriage and speech the broken-down actor fallen on evil days but nevertheless and always actor. Throughout the Prologue, from the moment when they mount the side-show stage, they jockey for position, gesture, work themselves up into theatrical flights and rhetorical emotions, play to each other as though they had an actual audience before them in the empty dark.

Mr. Zuss: This is it.

Nickles: This is what?

Mr. Zuss: Where they play the play, Horatio!

Nickles: Bare stage?

Mr. Zuss: Not in the least.
Heaven and earth. That platform's Heaven.

They step up onto the stage together.

3

Nickles: Looks like Heaven!

Mr. Zuss: As you remember it?

Nickles: Somebody's got to. You weren't there.
              They never sold balloons in Heaven —
              Not in my time.

Mr. Zuss: Only popcorn.

Nickles shrugs a shudder of disgust, heaving his tray.

Nickles: The two best actors in America
              Selling breath in bags . . .

Mr. Zuss: and bags
              To butter breath with . . .

Nickles: when they sell.

Mr. Zuss: Merchandise not moving, Nickles?

Nickles: Moves wherever I do — all of it.
              No rush to buy your worlds, I notice.

Mr. Zuss: I could sell one to a . . .

Nickles: . . . child!
              You told me. Where's the earth?

Mr. Zuss: Earth?
              Earth is where that table is:

4

That's where Job sits — at the table.
God and Satan lean above.

Mr. Zuss peers anxiously up into the canvas sky.

I wonder if we'd better?

Nickles: What?

Mr. Zuss: Play it.

Nickles: Why not? Who cares? *They* don't.

Mr. Zuss: At least we're actors. They're not actors.
Never acted anything.

Nickles: That's right.
They only own the show.

Mr. Zuss: ·   I wonder...

Nickles: They won't care and they won't know.

His eyes follow Mr. Zuss's up to the dangling bulbs.

Those stars that stare their stares at me —
Are those the staring stars I see
Or only lights...
              not meant for me?

Mr. Zuss: What's that got to do with anything?

Nickles: Very little. Shall we start?

Mr. Zuss: You think we ought to?

Nickles: They won't care.

Mr. Zuss: Let's start . . .
                 What staring stars?

Nickles: They aren't.
              They're only lights. Not meant.

Mr. Zuss: Why don't we
              Start?

Nickles: You'll play the part of . . .

Mr. Zuss: Naturally!

Nickles: Naturally! And your mask?

Mr. Zuss: ·   Mask!

Nickles: Mask. Naturally. You wouldn't play God in your
              Face would you?

Mr. Zuss: What's the matter with it?

Nickles: God the Creator of the Universe?
              God who hung the world in time?
              You wouldn't hang the world in time
              With a two-days' beard on your chin or a pinky!
              Lay its measure! Stretch the line on it!

Mr. Zuss stares coldly at Nickles, unhitches his balloon belt with

6

magnificent deliberation, drops it, steps forward to the front of
the wooden stage, strikes an attitude.

Mr. Zuss: Whatsoever is under the whole
                   Heaven is mine!

Nickles: That's what I mean.
                   You need a mask.

Mr. Zuss: *heavy irony*   Perhaps a more
                   Accomplished actor . . .

Nickles: Kiss your accomplishments!
                   Nobody doubts your accomplishments — none
                       of them —
                   The one man for God in the theater!
                   They'd all say that. Our ablest actor.
                   Nobody else for the part, they'd say.

Mr. Zuss: You make me humble.

Nickles: No! I'm serious.
                   The part was written for you.

Mr. Zuss: *gesture of protest*   Oh!

Nickles: But this is God in *Job* you're playing:
                   God the Maker: God Himself!
                   Remember what He says? — the hawk
                   Flies by His wisdom! And the goats —
                   Remember the goats? He challenges Job with
                       them:

Dost thou know the time of the wild goats?
What human face knows time like that time?
You'd need a face of fur to know it.
Human faces know too much too little.

Mr. Zuss: *suspiciously*
          What kind of mask?

Nickles: You'll find one somewhere.
        They never play without the masks.

Mr. Zuss: It's God the Father I play — not
          God the boiling point of water!

Nickles: Nevertheless the mask is imperative.
          If God should laugh
          The mare would calf
          The cow would foal:
          Diddle my soul . . .

Mr. Zuss: *shocked*
          God never laughs! In the whole Bible!

Nickles: That's what I say. *We* do.

Mr. Zuss: *I* don't.

Nickles: *Job* does. He covers his mouth with his hand.

Mr. Zuss: Job is abashed.

Nickles: He says he's abashed.

Mr. Zuss: He should be abashed: it's rank irreverence —
             Job there on the earth . . .

Nickles: On his dung heap . . .

Mr. Zuss: Challenging God!

Nickles: Crying to God.

Mr. Zuss: Demanding *justice* of *God!*

Nickles: Justice!
             No wonder he laughs. It's ridiculous. All of it.
             God has killed his sons, his daughters,
             Stolen his camels, oxen, sheep,
             Everything he has and left him
             Sick and stricken on a dung heap —
             Not even the consciousness of crime to comfort
                him —
             The rags of reasons.

Mr. Zuss: God is reasons.

Nickles: For the hawks, yes. For the goats. They're
                grateful.
             Take their young away they'll sing
             Or purr or moo or splash — whatever.
             Not for Job though.

Mr. Zuss: And that's why.

Nickles: Why what?

| Mr. Zuss: | He suffers. |

| Nickles: | Ah? Because he's ...
Not a bird you mean? |

| Mr. Zuss: | You're frivolous ... |

| Nickles: | That's precisely what you do mean!
The one thing God can't stomach is a man,
That scratcher at the cracked creation!
That eyeball squinting through into His Eye,
Blind with the sight of Sight! |

Nickles tugs himself free of his tray.

Blast this ...

| Mr. Zuss: | God created the whole world.
Who is Job to ... |

| Nickles: | Agh! the world!
The dirty whirler! The toy top! |

Mr Zuss: *kicking savagely at the popcorn tray and the balloon belt to shove them under the platform*
What's so wrong with the world?

| Nickles: | Wrong with it!
Try to spin one on a dung heap! |

Mr. Zuss does not answer. He goes on kicking at the tray.

Nickles sits on a rung of the ladder. After a time he begins to sing to himself in a kind of tuneless tune.

Nickles: I heard upon his dry dung heap
That man cry out who cannot sleep:
"If God is God He is not good,
If God is good He is not God;
Take the even, take the odd,
I would not sleep here if I could
Except for the little green leaves in the wood
And the wind on the water."

There is a long silence.

Mr. Zuss: You are a bitter man.

Nickles: *pompously*   ⌐I taste of the world!⌐
I've licked the stick that beat my brains out:
Stock that broke my father's bones!

Mr. Zuss: Our modern hero! Our Odysseus
Sailing sidewalks toward the turd
Of truth and touching it at last in triumph!
The honest, disillusioned man!
You sicken me.

Nickles: *hurt*   All right, I sicken you.
No need to be offensive, is there?
If you would rather someone else...

Mr. Zuss: Did what?

Nickles: Played Job.

Mr. Zuss:	What's Job to do with it?

Nickles: Job was honest. He saw God —
Saw him by that icy moonlight,
By that cold disclosing eye
That stares the color out and strews
Our lives . . . with light . . . for nothing.

Mr. Zuss: Job!
I never thought of you for Job.

Nickles: You never thought of me for Job!
What did you think of?

Mr. Zuss: Oh, there's always
Someone playing Job.

Nickles: There must be
Thousands! What's that got to do with it?
Thousands — not with camels either:
Millions and millions of mankind
Burned, crushed, broken, mutilated,
Slaughtered, and for what? For thinking!
For walking round the world in the wrong
Skin, the wrong-shaped noses, eyelids:
Sleeping the wrong night wrong city —
London, Dresden, Hiroshima.
There never could have been so many
Suffered more for less. But where do
I come in?

Mr. Zuss shuffles uncomfortably.

Play the dung heap?

Mr. Zuss:	All we have to do is start.
	Job will join us. Job will be there.
Nickles:	I know. I know. I know. I've seen him.
	Job is everywhere we go,
	His children dead, his work for nothing,
	Counting his losses, scraping his boils,
	Discussing himself with his friends and
	physicians,
	Questioning everything — the times, the stars,
	His own soul, God's providence.
	What do *I* do?
Mr. Zuss:	What do *you* do?
Nickles:	What do I do? You play God.
Mr. Zuss:	I play God. I think I mentioned it.
Nickles:	You play God and I play . . .

He lets himself down heavily on the rung of the ladder.

Ah!

Mr. Zuss: *embarrassed*
I had assumed you knew.

Nickles looks up at him, looks away.

Mr. Zuss:
You see,
I think of you and me as . . . opposites.

13

Nickles: Nice of you.

Mr. Zuss: I didn't mean to be nasty.

Nickles: Your opposite! A demanding role!

Mr. Zuss: I know.

Nickles: But worthy of me? Worthy of me!

Mr. Zuss: I have offended you. I didn't mean to.

Nickles: Did I say I was offended?

There is an awkward silence. Nickles, his face in his hands, begins to hum the tune to his little song. Mr. Zuss looks up and around into the corners of the sky, his head moving cautiously. At length Nickles begins to sing the words.

            I heard upon his dry dung heap
            That man cry out who cannot sleep:
            "If God is God He is not good,
            If God is good He is not God;
            Take the even, take the odd,
            I would not sleep here if I could ... "

Silence.

            So I play opposite to God!

Silence.

            Father of Lies they call me, don't they?

14

Mr. Zuss does not answer. He is still searching the dark above.
Silence. Nickles goes back to the song.

> "I would not sleep here if I could
> Except for the little green leaves in the wood
> And the wind on the water."

Silence. Then suddenly, theatrically, Nickles is on his feet.

> Who knows enough to know they're lies?
> Show me the mask!

Mr. Zuss: What mask?

Nickles: *attitude*   My mask!

Mr. Zuss: Are you sure you wear a mask?

Nickles: Meaning only God should wear one?

Mr. Zuss: Meaning are you sure it's there.

Nickles: They never play without them.

Mr. Zuss: Yes but
            Where?

Nickles: Where? In Heaven probably:
            Up on the platform there in Heaven!

Mr. Zuss: Yes ... You wouldn't care to ...

Nickles: What?

Mr. Zuss:	Find it for yourself?
Nickles:	In Heaven? Heaven is your department, Garrick.
Mr. Zuss:	My department! I suppose it is. Here! Hold this! Hold it! Steady...

Nickles steadies the ladder. Mr. Zuss climbs warily, keeping his eye on the canvas darkness; heaves himself over the rail; rummages around on the platform; turns, holding out a huge white, blank, beautiful, expressionless mask with eyes lidded like the eyes of the mask in Michelangelo's Night.

Nickles:	That's not mine — not *his*. It's His. I've known that face before. I've seen it. They find it under bark of marble Deep within the rinds of stone: God the Creator ...(*nastily*) of the animals!
Mr. Zuss: *outraged*	God of Everything that is or can!
Nickles:	Is or can — but cannot know.
Mr. Zuss:	There is nothing those closed eyes Have not known and seen.
Nickles:	Except To know they see: to know they've seen it. Lions and dolphins have such eyes. They know the way the wild geese know — Those pin-point travelers who go home To Labradors they never meant to,

16

Unwinding the will of the world like string.
What would they make of a man, those eyelids?

Mr. Zuss: Make of him! They *made* him.

Nickles: Made him
Animal like any other
Calculated for the boughs of
Trees and meant to chatter and be grateful!
But womb-worm wonders and grows wings —

Nickles breaks off, struck by his own words, goes on:

It actually does! The cock-eyed things
Dream themselves into a buzz
And drown on windowpanes. He made them
Wingless but they learn to wish.
That's why He fumbles Job. Job wishes! —
Thinks there should be justice somewhere —
Beats his bones against the glass.
Justice! In this cesspool! Think of it!
Job knows better when it's over.

Mr. Zuss: Job knows justice when it's over.
Justice has a face like this.

Nickles: Like blinded eyes?

Mr. Zuss: Like skies.

Nickles: Of stone.
Show me the other.

Mr. Zuss ducks away, rummaging in the clutter on the platform; turns again.

Mr. Zuss: You won't find it
                    Beautiful, you understand.

Nickles: I know that.
                    Beauty's the Creator's bait,
                    Not the Uncreator's: his
                    Is Nothing, the no-face of Nothing
                    Grinning with its not-there eyes.
                    Nothing at all! Nothing ever! . . .
                    Never to have been at all!

Mr. Zuss turns, lifts the second mask above Nickles' gesturing. This is large as the first but dark to the other's white, and open-eyed where the other was lidded. The eyes, though wrinkled with laughter, seem to stare and the mouth is drawn down in agonized disgust.

Mr. Zuss: Well?

Nickles is silent.

Mr. Zuss: *cheerfully*
                        That's it.

Silence.

                        You don't care for it?
                    It's not precisely the expression
                    Anyone would choose. I know that.
                    ⌈Evil is never very pretty: ⌉
                    ⌊Spitefulness either.⌋ Nevertheless it's

18

His — you'll grant that, won't you? — the
    traditional
Face we've always found for him anyway.
God knows where we go to find it:
Some subterranean memory probably.

Nickles has approached the ladder, staring. He does not reply.

Well, if you won't you won't. It's your
Option. I can't say I blame you.
I wouldn't do it. Fit my face to
That! I'd scrub the skin off afterward!
Eyes to those eyes!

Nickles: *harshly*   You needn't worry.
    Your beaux yeux would never bear that
    Look of . . .

Mr. Zuss: *smugly*   No. I know.

Nickles: . . . of pity!
    Let me have it.

*Nickles starts up the ladder, the mask in Mr. Zuss's hands
above him.*

                 Evil you call it!
Look at those lips: they've tasted something
Bitter as a broth of blood
And spat the sup out. Was that evil?

He climbs another rung.

    Was it?

Another rung.

> Spitefulness you say:
> You call that grin of anguish spite?

He pulls himself over the rail, takes the mask in his hands.

> I'd rather wear this look of loathing
> Night after night than wear that other
> Once — that cold complacence . . .

Mr. Zuss has picked up the first mask again, lifts it.

Nickles: Horrible!
> Horrible as a star above
> A burning, murdered, broken city!
> I'll play the part! . . .
>   Put your mask on! . . .
> Give me the lines! . . .

Mr. Zuss: What lines?

Nickles: His!
> Satan's!

Mr. Zuss: They're in the Bible aren't they?

Nickles: We're supposed to speak the Bible?

Mr. Zuss: *They* do . . .

*The light bulbs fade out, yellow to red to gone. A slow, strong
glow spots the platform throwing gigantic shadows up across the
canvas. Back to back the shadows of Mr. Zuss and Nickles ad-*

just their masks. The masked shadows turn to each other and gravely bow. Their gestures are the stiff formal gestures of pantomime. Their voices, when they speak, are so magnified and hollowed by the masks that they scarcely seem their own.

Godmask: Whence comest thou?

Satanmask: From going to and fro in the earth

There is a snicker of suppressed laughter.

        And from walking up and down in it . . .

A great guffaw. Mr. Zuss tears off his mask.

Mr. Zuss: *shouting*   Lights!

The spotlight fades out. The dangling bulbs come feebly on.

        Nobody told you to laugh like that.
        What's so funny? It's irreverent. It's impudent.
        After all, you are talking to God.
        That doesn't happen every Saturday
        Even to kitchen kin like you.
        Take that face off! It's indecent!
        Makes me feel like scratching somewhere!

Nickles painfully removes his mask.

Nickles: Do I look as though I'd laughed?
        If you had seen what I have seen
        You'd never laugh again! . . .

He stares at his mask.

Weep either . . .

Mr. Zuss: You roared. I heard you.

Nickles: Those eyes *see*.

Mr. Zuss: Of course they see — beneath the trousers
Stalking up the pulpit stair:
Under the skirts at tea — wherever
Decent eyes would be ashamed to.
Why should you laugh at that?

Nickles: It isn't
That! It isn't that at all!
They see the *world*. They do. They see it.
From going to and fro in the earth,
From walking up and down, they see it.
I know what Hell is now — to *see*.
Consciousness of consciousness . . .

Mr. Zuss: Now
Listen! This is a simple scene.
I play God. You play Satan.
God is asking where you've been.
All you have to do is tell him:
Simple as that. "In the earth," you answer.

Nickles: *Satan* answers.

Mr. Zuss: All right — Satan.
What's the difference?

Nickles: Satan *sees*.
          He sees the parked car by the plane tree.
          He sees behind the fusty door,
          Beneath the rug, those almost children
          Struggling on the awkward seat —
          Every impossible delighted dream
          She's ever had of loveliness, of wonder,
          Spilled with her garters to the filthy floor.
          Absurd despair! Ridiculous agony!

He looks at the mask in his hands.

          What has any man to laugh at!
          The panting crow by the dry tree
          Drags dusty wings. God's mercy brings
          The rains — but not to such as he.

Mr. Zuss: You play your part, I'll say that for you.
          In it or out of it, you play.

Nickles: You really think I'm playing?

Mr. Zuss: Aren't you?
          Somebody is. Satan maybe.
          Maybe Satan's playing *you*.
          Let's begin from the beginning.
          Ready!

They take their places back to back.

                    Masks!

They raise their masks to their faces.

Lights!

The bulbs go out. Darkness. Silence. In the silence:

A Distant Voice: Whence comest thou?

Mr. Zuss: That's my line.

Nickles: I didn't speak it.

Mr. Zuss: You did. Stop your mischief, won't you?

Nickles: Stop your own! Laughing. Shouting.

Mr. Zuss: Lights, I said!

The spotlight throws the enormous shadows on the canvas sky.

Godmask: Whence comest thou?

Satanmask: From going to and fro in the earth ...

A choked silence.

                    And from walking up and down in it.

Godmask: Hast thou considered my servant Job
                That there is none like him on the earth
                A perfect and an upright man, one
                That feareth God and escheweth evil?

*The platform lights sink, the masked shadows fading with
them, as a strong light comes on below isolating the table where
J.B. stands with his wife and children.*

24

SCENE ONE

The Platform is in darkness, the Table in light. J.B., a big, vigorous man in his middle or late thirties, stands at one end. At the other stands his wife, Sarah, a few years younger than her husband, a fine woman with a laughing, pretty face but a firm mouth and careful eyes, all New England. She is looking reprovingly but proudly at her five blond sons and daughters, who shift from foot to foot behind their chairs, laughing and nudging each other: David, 13; Mary, 12; Jonathan, 10; Ruth, 8; Rebecca, 6. Two buxom, middle-aged maids in frilly aprons stand behind with their hands folded. The children subside under their mother's eyes.

Sarah: J.B. . . .

The heads bow.

J.B.:   Our Father which art in Heaven
                  Give us this day our daily bread.

Rebecca and Ruth: *pulling their chairs out, clattering into them*
          Amenamen.

The Older Children: *less haste but no less eagerness*
                  Amen!

The Maids: *wheeling majestically but urgently to go out*
                  Amen!

Sarah: *to J.B. over the rattle of dishes and the clatter of talk as
    she sits down*
          That was short and sweet, my darling.

J.B.: *sitting down*
          What was?

Sarah: Grace was.

J.B.: *cheerfully*   All the essentials.

Sarah: Give? Eat?

J.B.:   Besides they're hungry.

Sarah: That's what grace is for — the hunger.
              Mouth and meat by grace amazed,
              God upon my lips is praised.

J.B.:   You think they stand in need of it — grace?
              Look at them!

Sarah: *beaming*   Yes! Look! Oh look!

*The maids parade in with a huge turkey on a silver platter, china
serving dishes with domed, blue covers, a gravy boat, a bottle of
wine in a napkin.*

Mary: Papá! Papá! He heard! He heard!

David: Who did?

Ruth: Ourfatherwhichartinheaven.

26

J.B.: *nudging the bird gently with his finger*
> He did indeed. What a bird He sent us!
> Cooked to a turn!

Ruth: He heard! He heard!

Jonathan: He heard! He heard! He sent a bird!

Sarah: That's enough now, children. Quiet!
>   Your father's counting.

J.B.:   Not today.
>   Not this gobbler. Feed a regiment.
>   Know what I was thinking, Sally?

Sarah: What?

J.B.:   How beautiful you are.

Sarah: With your eye on a turkey? I like that!

J.B.:   Why not? It's an eye-filling bird. Just look at it.

Sarah: Someday you might look at *me*.

J.B.:   I'm always looking at you, Sarah.

He rises, knife and steel in hand, clashing them against each other in a noble rhythm.

>   Everywhere I look I see you.

Sarah: *scornfully*
>   You never even see my clothes.

27

J.B.: *a shout of laughter*
    It's true. I don't. But I see *you.*

Sarah: *mock indignation*
    J! B!

J.B.:   And what's wrong with the turkey?
        What's wrong with that bottle of wine, either —
        Montrachet or I'll drink the whole of it!
        What's wrong with the bird or the wine or with
            anything —
        The day either — what's wrong with the day?

He begins carving expertly and rapidly.

        Tell me what day it is.

Jonathan: Turkey Day.

Mary: Cranberry Day.

Ruth: Succotash Day.

David: When we all can have white.

Jonathan: And giblets to bite.

Ruth: And two kinds of pie.

Jonathan: And squash in your eye.

Mary: And mashed potatoes with puddles of butter.

Jonathan: And gravy and such.

28

Rebecca: . . . and . . . and . . .

The children are screaming with laughter.

Sarah: Children!

Jonathan: *gasping*   And all eat too much.

Sarah: Children!
               Quiet! Quiet every one of you or
               Kate will take it all — everything —
               Knives, forks, turkey, glasses . . .

J.B.:   Not the wine though.

Sarah: Job, I'm serious.
               Answer your father's question, Jonathan.
               Tell him what day it is.

Jonathan: *hushed*   Thanksgiving.

Sarah: What day is that?

Jonathan: Thanksgiving Day.

David: The Day we give thanks to God.

Mary: For His goodness.

Sarah: And did you, David? Did you, Mary?
               Has any one of you thanked God?
               Really thanked Him?

There is an awkward silence.

Thanked Him for everything?

The children's heads are down. J.B. busies himself with his carving.

Sarah: *gently*   God doesn't give all this for nothing:
                A good home, good food,
                Father, mother, brothers, sisters.
                We too have our part to play.
                If we do our part He does His,
                He always has. If we forget Him
                He will forget. Forever. In everything.
                David!

David raises his head reluctantly.

                Did you think of God?

David does not reply.

                Did you think, when you woke in your beds this
                    morning,
                Any one of you, of Him?

Silence.

J.B.: *uncomfortable*
                Of course they did. They couldn't have helped
                    it . . .

                Bit of the breast for you, Rebecca?

Sarah: Please, Job. I want them to answer me.

J.B.: How can they answer things like that?

Gravy? That's the girl . . .

They know though.
Gift of waking, grace of light,
You and the world brought back together,
You from sleep, the world from night,
By God's great goodness and mercy . . .

Wing for Mary? Wing for Mary! . . .

They know all that. It's hard to talk about.

Sarah: *flushed, an edge to her voice*
Even if it's hard we have to.
We can't just take, just eat, just — relish!
Children aren't animals.

J.B.: *he goes on with his serving* Sweet Sal! Sweet Sal!
Children know the grace of God
Better than most of us. They see the world
The way the morning brings it back to them,
New and born and fresh and wonderful . . .

Ruth? She's always ravenous . . .

I remember . . .

Jonathan? He never is . . .

. . . when I was
Ten I used to stand behind

31

The window watching when the light began,
Hidden and watching.

                             That's for David —
Dark and thin.

Mary: Why? Why hidden?

J.B.:   Hidden from the trees of course.
              I must have thought the trees would see me
              Peeking at them and turn back.

Rebecca: Back where?

J.B.:   Back where they came from, baby.

              That's for your mother: crisp and gold.

Ruth: Father, you'd be cold. You didn't.

Sarah: *the edge still there*
              He still does. He lies there watching
              Long before I see the light —
              Can't bear to miss a minute of it:
              Sun at morning, moon at night,
              The last red apple, the first peas!
              I've never seen the dish he wouldn't
              Taste and relish and want more of:
              People either!

J.B.: *serving himself with heaping spoons*
                    Come on, Sal!
              Plenty of people I don't like.

He sits down. Pours himself a glass of wine.

I like their being people though . . .

Sips his wine.

Trying to be.

Sarah: You're hungry for them —
Any kind. People and vegetables:
Any vegetables so long as
Leaves come out on them. He loves leaves!

J.B.:   You love them too. You love them better.
Just because you know their names
You think you choose among your flowers:
Well, you don't. You love the lot of them.

Sarah: I can't take them as a gift though:
I owe for them. We do. We *owe*.

J.B.:   Owe for the greening of the leaves?

Sarah: Please!
Please, Job. I want the children
Somehow to understand this day, this . . .
Feast . . .

Her voice breaks.

J.B.:   Forgive me, Sal. I'm sorry — but
they
Do. They understand. A little.
Look at me, all of you.

              Ruth, you answer:

Why do we eat all this, these dishes,
All this food?

Ruth twists her napkin.

                  You say, Rebecca.
You're the littlest of us all.
Why?

Rebecca: Because it's good?

Sarah: Baby!
Ah, my poor baby!

J.B.:   Why your poor baby?
She's right, isn't she? It is. It's good.

Sarah: Good — and God has sent it to us!

J.B.:   She knows that.

Sarah: Does she?

She raises her head sharply.

                      Job! ...

                           do *you?*

Their eyes meet; hers drop.

        Oh, I think you do ...

                   but sometimes —

Times like this when we're together —
I get frightened, Job . . .

                                      we have so
Much!

J.B.: *dead serious*   You ought to think I do.
                Even if no one else should, you should.
                Never since I learned to tell
                My shadow from my shirt, not once,
                Not for a watch-tick, have I doubted
                God was on my side, was good to me.
                Even young and poor I knew it.
                People called it luck: it wasn't.
                I never thought so from the first
                Fine silver dollar to the last
                Controlling interest in some company
                I couldn't get — and got. It isn't
                Luck.

Mary: That's in the story.

Jonathan: Tell the
Story.

Ruth: Tell the lucky story.

Rebecca: Lucky, lucky, tell the lucky.

J.B.: *getting to his feet again to carve*
                Tell the story?

                        Drumstick, David?

Man enough to eat a drumstick?
You too, Jonathan?

Rebecca: Story, story.

J.B.:   Fellow came up to me once in a restaurant:
"J.B.," he says — I knew him . . .

Mary, want the other wing?

"Why do you get the best of the rest of us?"
Fellow named Foley, I think, or Sullivan:
New-come man he was in town.

Mary: Your turn, Mother.

Sarah: Patrick Sullivan.

J.B. and the children: *together in a shouted chant*
Patrick Sullivan, that's the man!

J.B.:   "Why do you get the best of the rest of us?
I've got as many brains as you.
I work as hard. I keep the lamp lit.
Luck! That's what it is," says Sullivan.
"Look!" I said. "Look out the window!"
"What do you see?" "The street," he tells me.

J.B. and the children: *as before*
"The street?" says I. "The street," says he.

J.B.:   "What do you want me to call it?" he asks me.
"What do I want you to call it?" says I.

36

"A road," says I. "It's going somewhere."
"Where?" says he. "You say," I said to him.

J.B. and the children:
    "God knows!" says Mr. Sullivan.

J.B.:   "He does," says I. "That's where it's going.
          That's where I go too. That's why."
          "Why what?" says he. "I get the best of you:
          It's God's country, Mr. Sullivan."

J.B. and the children:
    "God forbid!" says Mr. Sullivan.

J.B.:   I laughed till I choked. He only looked at me.
          "Lucky so-and-so," he yells.

Sarah: Poor Mr. Sullivan.

J.B.: *soberly*   He was wrong.
       It isn't luck when God is good to you.
       It's something more. It's like those dizzy
       Daft old lads who dowse for water.
       They feel the alder twig twist down
       And know they've got it and they have:
       They've got it. Blast the ledge and water
       Gushes at you. And they knew.
       It wasn't luck. They knew. They felt the
       Gush go shuddering through their shoulders,
          huge
       As some mysterious certainty of opulence.
       They couldn't hold it. I can't hold it.

He looks at Sarah.

> I've always known that God was with me.
> I've tried to show I knew it — not
> Only in words.

Sarah: *touched* Oh, you have,
> I know you have. And it's ridiculous,
> Childish, and I shouldn't be afraid . . .
> Not even now when suddenly everything
> Fills to overflowing in me
> Brimming the fulness till I feel
> My happiness impending like a danger.
> If ever anyone deserved it, you do.

J.B.: That's not true. I don't deserve it.
> It's not a question of deserving.

Sarah: Oh, it is. That's all the question.
> However could we sleep at night . . .

J.B.: Nobody *deserves* it, Sarah:
> Not the world that God has given us.

There is a moment's strained silence, then J.B. is laughing.

J.B.: But I believe in it, Sal. I trust in it.
> I trust my luck — my life — our life —
> God's goodness to me.

Sarah: *trying to control her voice* Yes! You do!
> I know you do! And that's what frightens me!
> It's not so simple as all that. It's not.

They mustn't think it is. God punishes.
God rewards and God can punish.
God is just.

J.B.: *easy again*   Of course He's just.
He'll never change. A man can count on Him.
Look at the world, the order of it,
The certainty of day's return
And spring's and summer's: the leaves' green —
That never cheated expectation.

Sarah: *vehemently*
God can reward and God can punish.
Us He has rewarded. Wonderfully.
Given us everything. Preserved us.
Kept us from harm, each one — each one.
And why? Because of you...

J.B. *raises his head sharply.*

Sarah: No!
Let me say it! Let me say it!
I need to speak the words that say it —
I need to hear them spoken. Nobody,
Nobody knows of it but me.
You never let them know: not anyone —
Even your children. They don't know.

J.B. *heaves himself out of his chair, swings round the table, leans over Sarah, his arms around her.*

J.B.:   Eat your dinner, Sal my darling.
We love our life because it's good:

It isn't good because we love it —
Pay for it — in thanks or prayers. The thanks are
Part of love and paid like love:
Free gift or not worth having.
You know that, Sal...

He kisses her.

                  better than anyone.
Eat your dinner, girl! There's not a
Harpy on the roof for miles.

She reaches up to touch his cheek with her hand.

Sarah: Nevertheless it's true, Job. You
Can trust your luck because you've earned the
Right to trust it: earned the right
For all of us to trust it.

J.B.: *back at his own place, filling his glass again*
                  Nonsense!
We get the earth for nothing, don't we?
It's given to us, gift on gift:
Sun on the floor, airs in the curtain.
We lie a whole day long and look at it
Crowing or crying in our cribs:
It doesn't matter — crow or cry
The sun shines, the wind blows...

Rebecca! Back for more already?

Rebecca: I want the wishbone please.

J.B.:   Whatever
        For?

Rebecca: To wish.

Sarah: For what, my baby?

Rebecca: For the wishbone.

Sarah: *pulling Rebecca into her lap*
                                Little pig!
                Wishing for wishes!

J.B.: *forking the wishbone onto Rebecca's plate*
                                That's my girl!

Sarah: She is! The spit and image of you!
                Thinking she can eat the world
                With luck and wishes and no thanks!

J.B.:   That isn't fair. We're thankful, both of us.

Sarah: *cuddling Rebecca*
                Both! And both the same! Just look at you!
                A child shows gratitude the way a woman
                Shows she likes a pretty dress —
                Puts it on and takes it off again —
                That's the way a child gives thanks:
                She tries the world on. So do you.

J.B.:   God understands that language, doesn't He?
                He should. He made the colts.

Sarah:	But you're not
	Colts! You talk. With tongues. Or ought to.
J.B.:	And we use them, don't we, baby?
	We love Monday, Tuesday, Wednesday...
Sarah: *rocking Rebecca on her knees*
	We love Monday, Tuesday, Wednesday.
	Where have Monday, Tuesday, gone?
	Under the grass tree,
	Under the green tree,
	One by one.
Jonathan:	Say it again, Mother ... Mother!
Sarah:	I never said it before. I don't
	Know ...
	How would you think it would go?
	How does it go, Job? You said it.
J.B.:	I didn't. I said we loved the world:
	Monday, Tuesday, Wednesday, all of it.
Sarah:	How would you think it would go, Jonathan?

The words fall into a little tune as she repeats them.

I love Monday, Tuesday, Wednesday.
Where have Monday, Tuesday, gone?
Under the grass tree,
Under the green tree,
One by one.

Caught as we are in Heaven's quandary,
Is it they or we are gone
Under the grass tree,
Under the green tree?

I love Monday, Tuesday, Wednesday.
One by one.

Rebecca: *drowsily*   Say it again.

Sarah: Say it again?

Jonathan: You say it, Father.

J.B.:   To be, become, and end are beautiful.

Rebecca: That's not what she said at all.

J.B.:   Isn't it? Isn't it?

Sarah: *kissing her*   Not at all.

The light fades, leaving the two shadows on the canvas sky.

SCENE TWO

The Platform. As the platform light comes on, the figures fade from the canvas sky and Mr. Zuss and Nickles straighten up, lifting their masks off, stretching, yawning.

Mr. Zuss: Well, that's our pigeon.

Nickles: Lousy actor.

Mr. Zuss: Doesn't really act at all.

Nickles: Just eats.

Mr. Zuss: And talks.

Nickles: The love of life!
Poisoning their little minds
With love of life! At that age!

Mr. Zuss: No!
Some of that, I thought, was beautiful.

Nickles: Best thing you can teach your children
Next to never drawing breath
Is choking on it.

Mr. Zuss: Who said that?
Someone's spoiled philosophy, it sounds like:

44

Intellectual butter a long war
And too much talking have turned rancid.
I thought he made that small familiar
Feast a true thanksgiving . . . only . . .

Nickles: Only what?

Mr. Zuss: Something went wrong.

Nickles: That's what I've been telling you.

Mr. Zuss: He didn't
Act.

Nickles: He can't. He's not an actor.

Mr. Zuss: I wonder if he knows?

Nickles: Knows what?

Mr. Zuss: Knows that he's in it?

Nickles: Is he?

Mr. Zuss: Certainly.

Nickles: How can you tell?

Mr. Zuss: That's him. That's Job.
He has the wealth, the wife, the children,
Position in the world.

Nickles: The piety!

45

Mr. Zuss:	He loves God, if that's what you're saying. *A perfect and an upright man.*
Nickles:	Piety's hard enough to take Among the poor who *have* to practice it. A rich man's piety stinks. It's insufferable.
Mr. Zuss:	You're full of fatuous aphorisms, aren't you! A poor man's piety is hope of having: A rich man *has* his — and he's grateful.
Nickles:	Bought and paid for like a waiter's smirk! You know what talks when that man's talking? All that gravy on his plate — His cash — his pretty wife — his children! Lift the lot of them, he'd sing Another canticle to different music.
Mr. Zuss:	That's what Satan says — but better.
Nickles:	It's obvious. No one needs to say it.
Mr. Zuss:	You don't like him.
Nickles:	I don't have to. You're the one who has to like him.
Mr. Zuss:	I thought you spoke of Job with sympathy.
Nickles:	Job on his dung hill, yes. That's human. That makes sense. But this world-master, This pious, flatulent, successful man Who feasts on turkey and thanks God! — He sickens me!

46

Mr. Zuss: Of course he sickens you,
            He trusts the will of God and loves —

*Mr. Zuss is swollen with indignation and rhetoric. He swoops
his mask up from the rail with a magnificent gesture, holds it.*

            Loves a woman who must sometime, some-
                where,
            Later, sooner, leave him; fixes
            All his hopes on little children
            One night's fever or a running dog
            Could kill between the dark and day;
            Plants his work, his enterprise, his labor,
            Here where every planted thing
            Fails in its time but still he plants it . . .

Nickles: *nastily*
            God will teach him better won't He?
            God will show him what the world is like —
            What man's like — the ignoble creature,
            Victim of the spinning joke!

Mr. Zuss: Teach him better than he knows!
            God will show him God!

Nickles: *shrugging*   It's the same
            Thing. It hurts.

Mr. Zuss: *gathering momentum*   God will teach him!
            God will show him what God *is* —
            Enormous pattern of the steep of stars,
            Minute perfection of the frozen crystal,
            Inimitable architecture of the slow,

47

                    Cold, silent, ignorant sea-snail:
                    The unimaginable will of stone:
                    Infinite mind in midge of matter!

Nickles: Infinite mush! Wait till your pigeon
                    Pecks at the world the way the rest do —
                    Backward: eager beak to naked bum!

Mr. Zuss: You ought to have your tongue torn out!

Nickles: All men should: to suffer silently.

Mr. Zuss: Get your mask back on! I tell you
                    Nothing this good man might suffer,
                    Nothing at all, would make him yelp
                    As you do. He'd praise God no matter.

Nickles: *whispering*
                    Why must he suffer then?

*The question catches Mr. Zuss with his mask halfway to his face.
He lowers it slowly, staring into it as though the answer might
be written inside.*

Mr. Zuss: *too loud*   To praise!

Nickles: *softly*
                    He praises now. Like a canary.

Mr. Zuss lifts his mask again.

Mr. Zuss: Well, will you put it on or won't you?

Nickles: Shall I tell you why?
       violently   To learn!
               Every human creature born
               Is born into the bright delusion
               Beauty and loving-kindness care for him.
               Suffering teaches! Suffering's good for us!
               Imagine men and women dying
               Still believing that the cuddling arms
               Enclosed them! They would find the worms
               Peculiar nurses, wouldn't they? Wouldn't they?

He breaks off; picks his mask up; goes on in a kind of jigging chant half to himself.

               What once was cuddled must learn to kiss
               The cold worm's mouth. That's all the mystery.
               That's the whole muddle. Well, we learn it.
               God is merciful and we learn it . . .
               We learn to wish we'd never lived!

Mr. Zuss: This man will not.

Nickles: Won't he? Won't he?
               Shall I tell you how it ends?
               Shall I prophesy? I see our
               Smug world-master on his dung heap,
               Naked, miserable, and alone,
               Pissing the stars. Ridiculous gesture! —
               Nevertheless a gesture — meaning
               All there is on earth to mean:
               Man's last word . . . and worthy of him!

49

Mr. Zuss:	This man will not. He trusts God. No matter how it ends, he trusts Him.
Nickles:	Even when God tests him? — tortures him?
Mr. Zuss:	Would God permit the test unless He knew the outcome of the testing?
Nickles:	Then why test him if God knows?
Mr. Zuss:	So Job can see.
Nickles:	See what?
Mr. Zuss:	See God.
Nickles:	A fine sight from an ash heap, certainly!
Mr. Zuss:	Isn't there anything you understand? It's from the ash heap God is seen Always! Always from the ashes. Every saint and martyr knew that.
Nickles:	And so he suffers to see God: Sees God because he suffers. Beautiful!
Mr. Zuss:	Put on your mask. I'd rather look at . . .
Nickles:	I should think you would! A human Face would shame the mouth that said that!

They put their masks on fiercely, standing face to face. The platform light fades out. The spotlight catches them, throwing

*the two masked shadows out and up. The voices are magnified
and hollow, the gestures formal, as at the end of the Prologue.*

Godmask: Hast thou considered my servant Job
              That there is none like him on the earth,
              A perfect and an upright man, one
              That feareth God and escheweth evil?

Satanmask: *sardonic*
              Doth Job fear God for naught?

The God-shadow turns away in a gesture of anger.

Satanmask: *deprecatingly*
              Hast thou not made an hedge about him
              And about his house
              And about all that he hath on every side?
              Thou hast blessed the work of his hands
              And his substance is increased.

The voice drops.

              But put forth thine hand now and touch
              All that he hath . . .

The voice becomes a hissing whisper.

                              and he will
              Curse thee to thy face!

Godmask: *in a furious, great voice, arm thrown out in a gesture
         of contemptuous commitment*
              Behold!
              All that he hath is in thy power!

The Satan-shadow bows mockingly; raises its two arms, advancing until the shadows become one shadow. The light fades. Suddenly, out of the darkness the Distant Voice of the Prologue.

The Distant Voice:
>   Only . . .

Silence.

Godmask: Only
             Upon himself
             Put not forth thy hand!

Darkness. The crash of a drum; a single stroke. Silence.

> *Note: The play is conceived and written without breaks, but if recesses in the action are desired one might well be made at this point.*

SCENE THREE

The Table. As the lights come on the two leaning shadows, one thrown upon the other, are visible on the canvas sky. They fade as the scene brightens. The table has been pushed to one side as though against a window in a living room. Sarah stands before it arranging flowers in a bowl. J.B. is straddling a chair, watching.

Sarah: Look, Job! Look! Across the street.
                Two soldiers.

J.B.:   What about them?

Sarah: Only they
                Stare so.

J.B.:   Stare at what?

Sarah: The house.
                I think they're drunk . . . A little.

J.B. rises, stands beside her, his arm around her waist.

J.B.:   Plastered!

Sarah: One of them anyway. He wobbles.

J.B.:   That's no wobble. That's a waltz step.

53

Sarah:	They're crossing over.
J.B.:	They sure are.
Sarah:	What do you think they ...
J.B.:	Listen!
Sarah:	Yes ... What do you think they want, two soldiers?
J.B.:	No idea. Johnson will tend to them.
Sarah:	I've never seen such staring eyes.
J.B.:	Glazed. Just glazed.
Sarah:	They keep on ringing. I know what it is, J.B., They have some kind of message for us. David has sent them with a message — Something about his regiment. They're coming Every day now, ship by ship. I hear them in the harbor coming. He couldn't write and so he sent them.
J.B.:	Pretty drunk for messengers, those soldiers.
Sarah:	What does it matter. They're just boys. They've just got home. It doesn't matter.
J.B.:	Johnson's a judge of drunks. He'll handle them.
Sarah:	He mustn't send them off. Don't let him!

There is a commotion outside the canvas door. A voice, off.

Voice: Two young ... gentlemen to see you.
       Friends, they say, of Mr. David.

Sarah: Oh, I knew! I knew! I knew!

Voice (off): That's telling him, Puss-foot!

Voice (off):   Puss-face!

*The two Messengers enter, dressed as soldiers. The First is
flushed and loud; the Second, very drunk, pale as bone.*

J.B.:   Come in, gentlemen. Come in. Come in.
      David's friends are always welcome.
      This is David's mother.

Sarah: Won't you sit
     Down?

First Messenger: What did I tell you, Punk!
      Any friends of David's.

Second Messenger: Any at
     All ...

First M.:   I told you that boy meant it.
      What did I say when I see the joint?
      That's the number, Punk, I told you.
      Old Ten Twenty: that's the number.

He turns to Sarah.

Twenty if you're men, he told us —
Ten for horses' whatses. What the
Hell, he always said: we're friends.

Second M.:   Any at all he always ...

First M.:   Pardon the
Language, lady.

Second M.:   Any a' ...

Sarah: There!
Sit down.

First M.:   It's just, we saw the number.

Sarah: And David asked you to drop in.

First M.:   Any friend of his, he told us.
Any time.

Second M.:   And we were cold:
A cold, hard march ...

First M.:   What the
Hell's the matter with *you!* You drunk?

Sarah: Sit by the fire, both of you. Where was he?

First M.:   Where was who?

Sarah: David.

First M.:   When?

J.B.:   When he told you.

First M.:   In the mess.
              Any friend of his, he told us.
              Any time at all. Why?
              You think we're lying to you?

J.B.:   Certainly
              Not.

First M.:   You think we never knew him?

Sarah: Of course. Of course you do.

First M.:   We knew him.

Second M.:   Fumbling among the faces ... knew him ...
              Night ... our fingers numb ...

First M.:   Will you shut
              Up or will I clout you, Big Mouth!

To Sarah.

              That's why we come: because we knew him.
              To tell you how we knew him.

Sarah: Thank you.

57

Silence.

Second M.:   How it was with him ...

First M.:   Listen, Punk!

Second M.:   How, by night, by chance, darkling ...
By the dark of chance ...

First M.:   He's drunk.

Second M.:   How, the war done, the guns silent ...
No one knows who gave the order.

First M.: *raising his voice*
Like I say, because he said to.
Any friend of his he said to.
Just to tell you we knew David:
Maybe drink to David maybe ...

Sarah: Yes! Oh yes! Let's drink to David!
J.B.!

J.B.:   Bourbon? Scotch?

First M.:   Now you're
Cooking! Take your pants off, Punk:
We're in.

Sarah: That's right. Put your feet up.
Oh, they're not too dirty. David's are
Dirtier. I'm sure of that.

First M.:   David's feet! I'll say they are.
               Look! What's going on here! David's
               Feet!

Sarah: I meant — with all that marching.

First M.:   I don't get it. Look, it's true
               They didn't have the right length lumber:
               We did the best we could . . .

J.B. starts to his feet.

J.B.:   What in
               God's name are you saying, soldier?

Sarah: *rising*

               What does he mean, the lumber?

Silence.

First M.:   You don't
               Know? Ain't that the army for you!

To the Second Messenger.

               They don't know. They never told them.

Sarah: Told us what?

First M.:   We better go.

Sarah: No! Please! Please! No!

First M.:   Come on, we're getting out, you lunkhead.

J.B.:   Not until you've told me. Sarah!
                Perhaps you'd better, Sarah . . .

Sarah: Please,
                I want to hear it.

First M.:   Jesus! . . . Jesus! . . .

*There is a long silence. The Second Messenger turns slowly to
J.B., his face drunken white, his eyes blank.*

Second M.:   *I only am escaped alone to tell thee* . . .

*The focus of light opens to include the Platform where Mr. Zuss
and Nickles stand staring down, their masks in their hands. Mr.
Zuss's face is expressionless. Nickles wears a twisted grin. The
Second Messenger's head falls forward onto his knees.*

Second M.:   . . . My tongue loosened by drink . . .

                                        my thought
                Darkened as by wind the water . . .

                That day is lost where it befell . . .

Sarah: *she is holding herself by the straining of her clenched
       hands*
                What is it we were never told?

J.B.:   It isn't
                True you little drunken liar!
                It can't be true! It isn't possible!

60

Silence. The passion ebbs from J.B.'s voice.

We had a letter from him.

Silence. Then, uncertainly

After the
End of it we had a letter. . . .

Nickles jerks a crooked leg over the rail, starts awkwardly down the ladder, watching intently, peering back up at Mr. Zuss, watching.

Second M.:　What shall I say to you . . . ?

What I saw . . . ?

What I believe I saw . . . ?

Or what
I must have seen . . .

and have forgotten?

Sarah: *a cry*　David is our son, our son, our son.

Nickles: *prompting her from his ladder in a harsh half-whispeı*
That's the tune. He's *ours*. Go on with it:
Can't be happening to *us!* Can't be!
God won't let it happen, not to
Our kind, God won't!

He leers up at Mr. Zuss.

J.B.: *turning Sarah away from the Second Messenger into his
      arms*   Sarah! Sarah!
                David's all right. He has to be. He is.
                I know he is. The war is over.
                It never could have happened — never —
                Never in this world.

Nickles: *the whisper harsher*   Couldn't it?
                Ask him! Couldn't it? Suppose it did though:
                What would the world be made of then?

Second M.:   I only am escaped alone, companions
                Fallen, fallen, fallen . . .

                                    .   the earth
                Smell remembers that there was a man.

Sarah: Job! He's dead! God has taken him!

The focus of light narrows, is extinguished.

SCENE FOUR

*Darkness. Silence. Then the crash of a drum. Silence again.
Then two cigarettes are lighted, one high above the stage, one
lower. Then gradually the lights come on, making four circles
across the front of the stage like the circles of sidewalk brightness
under street lamps. Where the cigarettes were lighted Mr. Zuss
and Nickles are now visible on the platform rail and the ladder,
squatting there like two tramps on the stairs of a stoop, turning
their heads together one way and then the other, watching, not
speaking. After a time the First Messenger comes strolling in
from their right, a news camera slung from his neck. The Second
follows with a notebook. They wear battered felt hats with their
khaki shirts and trousers. They are followed at a little distance
by a stylishly dressed girl.*

Girl: I don't like it.

First Messenger: You'll do fine.

Girl: I wish I was home in bed with a good
Boy or something. I don't like it.

First M.:   You'll do fine.

Girl: I won't do fine:
I'm frightened.

First M.:   All you do, you go up to them,
Get them talking, keep them looking.

Girl:	Go up to them yourselves, why don't you?
First M.:	Sure, and get the brush-off. Girl like You can keep them talking; keep them Looking, that is. Pretty girl.
Girl:	I don't like it.
Second M.:	You'll get used to it.
Girl:	Not where I work. Not Society. Society page they never die. Girl gets asked. Girl gets married. Girl gets photographed in night club. Girl gets older. Girl gets off. Never catch them dead on Society.
Second M.:	Like the robins.
First M.:	Yeah, like robins.
Girl:	Why the robins?
Second M.:	Never see one Dead.
First M.:	Nor sparrows neither.
Second M.:	Either.
First M.:	Never hardly. Must be millions.
Second M.:	Hardly ever see one dead.

Girl:	What happens to them?
Second M.:	They get over it.
Girl:	Over what?
Second M.:	Over being there.
Girl:	All I know is I don't like it. Keep them talking till a flash bulb Smacks them naked in the face — It's horrible!
First M.:	It's genius! Listen, lady! How do I get the photograph without? Answer me that. How do I get the Look a mother's face has maybe Once in a lifetime: just before Her mouth knows, when her eyes are knowing?
Girl:	I can't do it.
First M.:	*She* can't do it! All you got to do is walk. Wiggle your can. Keep them looking. Then he tells them. Then I take them. Then you beat it. Then that's that. Except the drink we're going to buy you Payday evening if you're good — And if you're not there's lots of liars.

65

Second M.:   You don't have to tell them: I **do.**

Girl: Why do *you?*

Second M.:   Because I have to.
              I'm the one that has to tell them.

Girl: Why?

Second M.: *shrugging*
                    Oh . . .

Girl: Why?

Second M.:   There's always
              Someone has to tell them, isn't there?

Girl: Someone else can.

Second M.:   No. There's always . . .

He is groping from word to word.

              Someone chosen by the chance of seeing,
              By the accident of sight,
              By stumbling on the moment of it,
              Unprepared, unwarned, unready,
              Thinking of nothing, of his drink, his bed,
              His belly, and it happens, and he sees it . . .

He winces his eyes shut.

              Caught in that inextricable net

Of having witnessed, having seen . . .

He alone!

Girl: *gently*   But you don't have to.

To the First Messenger.

Why does he have to?

Second M.:   It was I.
I only. I alone. The moment
Closed us together in its gaping grin
Of horrible incredulity. I saw their
Eyes see mine! We *saw* each other!

First M.:   He has to. He was there. He saw it.
Route Two. Under the viaduct.
Traveling seventy — seventy-five —
Kid was driving them was drunk,
Had to be drunk, just drove into it.
He was walking home. He saw it.
Saw it start to, saw it had to,
Saw it. J.B.'s son. His daughter.
Four in all and all just kids.
They shrieked like kids he said.

Second M.:   Then silent.
Blond in all that blood that daughter.

Girl: *her voice rising*
He can't tell them *that!*

First M.:   He has to.
          Someone has to. They don't know.
          They been out all evening somewhere.

Girl: *hysterically*
          They don't have to know!

First M.:   They have to.

*Nickles and Mr. Zuss on their perches have seen something
off to their right. They turn their heads together.*

Girl: No!

First M.: *looking right, pulling his camera around*
                    That's them. They're coming. Quiet!

Girl: I can't do it.

First M.: *brutally*   You can do it.

*J.B. and Sarah, arm in arm, walk slowly into the first circle
of light. Nickles and Mr. Zuss lean forward, their masks
dangling from their hands.*

Second M.: *under his breath, staring at them as they come*
          I only, I alone, to tell thee . . .
          I who have understood nothing, have known
          Nothing, have been answered nothing . . .

Girl: *crossing to meet them with an affected walk, the First
          Messenger screening himself behind her, the Second fol-
          lowing*   Good
          Evening! What a pleasant evening!

Back from the theatre so soon?
We're neighbors, don't you know? You've met
    my
Miffkin walking me each morning:
You know Muff, my purple poodle . . .

Isn't it a pleasant evening!

Second M.:   I'm from the press. There's been an accident . . .

He falters.

First M.:   Four kids in a car. They're dead.
             Two were yours. Your son. Your daughter.
             Cops have got them in a cab.
             Any minute now they'll be here.

He raises his camera over the girl's shoulder.

Girl: *in her own voice, screaming*
             Don't look! Cover your face!

Sarah: *with scarcely the breath to say it*
             Mary . . . Jonathan . . .

The flash. J.B. throws his elbow up as if to ward off a blow.
Sarah does not move.

J.B.:   You bastards!
             I'll beat your god damned brains out . . .

He lunges after them blinded by the flash as they scatter.

                                            Where have you
          Gone?

*Sarah moves like a sleepwalker through the circles of light,
one after the other, touches a chair, goes down on her knees
beside it, clinging to it.*

J.B.:   Answer me!

Silence.

J.B.:   Answer me!

Silence.

Sarah: *her voice dead*   It wasn't
                 They that did it . . .

*J.B. comes slowly back out of the darkness, sees her, crosses
to her. There is a long silence, J.B. looking right and left along
the street.*

Sarah: Why did He do it to them?
          What had they done to Him — those chil-
          dren . . .
          What had they done to Him . . .

                                   and we —
          What had *we* done? . . .

                                   What had *we* done?

J.B.:   Don't, Sarah. Don't!

Nickles lights a cigarette, grins back over his shoulder to Mr.
Zuss in the handful of yellow glare.

J.B.:   It doesn't
                Help to think that.

Sarah: Nothing helps! . . .
                Nothing can help them now.

J.B.: *a clumsy gesture*   It . . . happened . . .

Sarah: *fiercely*
                Yes, and Who let it happen?

J.B.: *awkwardly*   Shall we . . .
                Take the good and not the evil?
                We have to take the chances, Sarah:
                Evil with good.
        then, in a desperate candor
                          It doesn't mean there
                Is no good!

Nickles: *in his cracked whisper*
                          Doesn't it? Doesn't it?

Mr. Zuss: *silencing Nickles with his hand, his whisper hardly*
        heard

                Go on! Go on! That path will lead you.

Sarah: *bitterly*
                When you were lucky it was God!

J.B.:   Sticks and stones and steel are chances.
         There's no will in stone and steel . . .

His voice breaks.

It happens to us . . .

He drops on his knees beside her.

Sarah: No! . . .

                                        Don't touch me!

She clings to the chair, motionless, not weeping.

The circles of light fade out.

SCENE FIVE

The dark diminishes until the white coats of Mr. Zuss and Nickles are visible on the platform. Mr. Zuss lifts a padded drumstick. Nickles balances on the rail and starts cautiously down the ladder.

Mr. Zuss: Ready?

Nickles: *cheerfully* Got to be, don't they?

Mr. Zuss: I meant
You.

Nickles: They've got no choice. Disaster —
Death — mankind are always ready —
Ready for anything that hurts.

Mr. Zuss: And you?

Nickles: I too! I too!

Mr. Zuss: Provided
Someone else will bleed the blood
And wipe the blinded eye?

Nickles: I watch
Your world go round!

Mr. Zuss: It must be wearing.

Nickles: Oh, it has its compensations.
Even a perfect and an upright man
Learns if you keep turning long enough.

First he thought it wasn't happening —
Couldn't be happening — not to him —
Not with you in the stratosphere tooting the
Blue trombone for the moon to dance.
Then he thought it chanced by chance!
a dry hiccup of laughter
        Childish hypothesis of course
But still hypothesis — a start —
A pair of tongs to take the toad by —
Recognition that it *is* a toad:
Not quite comfort but still comfortable,
Eases the hook in the gills a little:
He'll learn.

Mr. Zuss: *preoccupied*   Learn what?

Nickles: Your — purpose for him!

Mr. Zuss: Keep your tongue in your teeth, will you?

He notices Nickles' descent on the ladder for the first time.

        Here! Wait a minute! Wait a
Minute! Where are you off to?

Nickles: Bit of a
Walk in the earth for my health — or some-
    body's.
  bitterly
        Up and down in the earth, you know —
Back and forth in it . . .

Mr. Zuss: Leave him alone!

Nickles: He needs a helping hand: you've seen that —
A nudge from an old professional.

Mr. Zuss: Leave him a'
Lone! He can't act and you know it.

Nickles: He doesn't have to act. He suffers.
It's an old role — played like a mouth-organ.
Any idiot on earth
Given breath enough can breather it —
Given tears enough can weep.
All he needs is help to see.

Mr. Zuss: See what?

Nickles: That bloody drum-stick striking;
See Who lets it strike the drum!

*Mr. Zuss, whose lifted arm has been slowly falling, raises it
abruptly.*

Mr. Zuss: Wait!

He starts to strike the drum, stops the stroke in mid-air.

Wait for me. I'm coming.
Down!
Wait!
Wait I tell you!

The stroke of the drum. The light fades out.

Out of the dark two circles of light, one on the platform, one on the table. Behind the table are the two Messengers. The First, wearing a police sergeant's cap, sits on a chair. The Second, wearing a patrolman's cap, stands beside him. J.B., a raincoat over rumpled clothes, stands facing them. Above, on the platform, as on the landing of a stair, Sarah stands pulling a dressing gown around her shoulders. Nickles and Mr. Zuss, their masks in their hands, straddle a couple of chairs beyond the circle of light which centers on the table.

First M.:   Sorry to question you like this.
      We got to get the story.

J.B.: *impatiently*   Go on.

First M.:   Turning your house into a . . .

J.B.:   No. Go on.
      It doesn't matter.

Sarah: *toneless*   Nothing matters but to
     Know.

First M.:   How many children?

Silence.

J.B.:   Two.

First M.: *writing*
     Girls?

Sarah: We had two boys.

76

First M.: *writing*   Girls.
                 Names?

J.B.:   Ruth. Rebecca.

Sarah: Ruth is the
                 Oldest . . . now.

First M.·   And you last saw her?

J.B.:   Ruth?

Sarah: *her voice rising*
                 It's Rebecca is missing!

J.B.: *silencing her*   He
                 Knows!

Sarah: *harshly*   No, it's God that knows!

*There is an awkward silence. When Sarah speaks again her
voice is dead.*

                 She's the littlest one. She's gone.

First M.:   How long ago?

Sarah: Oh . . . hours!

First M.:   It's three in the morning now.

J.B.:   Since seven.

First M.: *writing*
          And you reported it?

J.B.:   Yes.

First M.:   When?

J.B.:   One o'clock. A quarter after.
          We looked for her everywhere, of course.
          Then we thought — I thought — if somebody . . .

          Maybe the telephone would ring.

First M.:   And you'd do better on your own?

J.B.: *reluctantly*
          Yes.

Sarah: *with rising violence*
                 Yes! Yes! Yes!
          We believe in our luck in this house!
          We've earned the right to! We believe in it . . .
     bitterly   All but the bad!

Nickles: *rocking back on his chair*
                     That's playing it!
          That's playing it!

He begins to sing in his cracked whisper, beating a jazzed rhythm on the back of his mask as though it were a banjo.

          If God is Will
          And Will is well

Then what is ill?
God still?
Dew tell!

Mr. Zuss does not seem to hear. He is listening intently to the scene at the table.

First M.:   And nobody telephoned?

J.B.:   Nobody telephoned.

First M.: *writing*   Dressed? How was she
          Dressed?

J.B.: *turning for the first time to look up at Sarah*
          White?

Sarah: White! You saw her
      Glimmering in the twilight.

First M.: *writing*   White.

Sarah: All but her
      Shoes.

The First Messenger looks up at the Second.

First M.:   Her shoes were what?

Sarah: Red.

The First Messenger looks up again. The Second turns his face away.

First M.:   Rebecca have a red umbrella?

Sarah: Parasol.

First M.:   Little toy umbrella.

Sarah: *startled*
          Parasol. Yes, she might have had one.

First M.:   You mean she owned one?

Sarah: Yes. It belonged to a
          Big doll we bought her once.
          Scarlet silk. It opens and closes.
          She kept it when the doll gave out.
          She used to take it to bed with her even —
          Open and close it.

*The First Messenger looks up for the third time at the Second,
whose face, still turned away, is like stone.*

J.B.: *a step forward*   You've found the parasol!

Second M.: *not looking at him; a voice without expression or
          tone*
          What will it tell you? Will it tell you why?

J.B.: *to First M.*
          I asked you: have you found the parasol?

First M.:   He's the one. Ask him. He'll tell you.

Second M.: *with difficulty, like a man speaking out of physical
          pain*

> Can the tooth among the stones make an-
> swer? . . .
>
> Can the seven bones reply? . . .
>
> Out in the desert in the tombs
> Are potter's figures: two of warriors,
> Two of worthies, two of camels,
> Two of monsters, two of horses.
> Ask them why. They will not answer you . . .

He brushes his hand heavily across his face.

> Death is a bone that stammers . . .
>
>   a tooth
> Among the flints that has forgotten.

J.B.: *violently*
> Ask him! Has he found the parasol!

First M.:
> We don't know. He found an umbrella —
> Doll's umbrella — red.

Sarah:
>   Oh, where?

J.B.:
> Nothing else? Just the umbrella?

First M.: *to Second*
> Tell them, will you!

The Second Messenger does not move or speak. The First shrugs, looks down at his pencil, rattles it off in a matter-of-fact monotone.

> Just past midnight
> Pounding his beat by the back of the lumberyard
> Somebody runs and he yells and they stumble —
> Big kid — nineteen maybe —
> Hopped to the eyes and scared — scared
> Bloodless he could barely breathe.
> Constable yanks him up by the britches:
> "All right! Take me to it!"
> Just a shot in the dark, he was so
> Goddam scared there had to be something . . .
>
> Well . . .
>
> He took him to it . . .
>
> back of the
> Lumber trucks beside the track.

J.B.: Go on.

First M.: She had a toy umbrella.
     That was all she had — but shoes:
     Red shoes and a toy umbrella.
     It was tight in her fist when he found her — still.

J.B.: Let me see it! The umbrella!

First M.: Constable will show it to you.

The Second Messenger takes something wound in newspaper out of his pocket. He does not look at it or them. The First Messenger half opens it, lays it on the table.

82

Sarah: Oh, my baby! Oh, my baby!

The First Messenger gets out of his chair, stands a moment awkwardly, goes out. The Second follows. J.B. stands motionless over the table. Sarah hugs her dressing gown around her, rocking herself slowly, her head bowed.

Nickles: *leaning forward toward J.B., a wheedling whisper*
          Now's the time to say it, mister.

Mr. Zuss: Leave him alone!

J.B.: *touching the parasol*   The Lord giveth ...

His voice breaks.

                                              the
          Lord taketh away!

Mr. Zuss: *rising, whispering*   Go on!
          Go on! Finish it! Finish it!

Nickles: What should he
          Finish when he's said it all?

Mr. Zuss: Go on!

Nickles: To what? To where? He's got there, hasn't he?
          Now he's said it, now he knows.
          He knows Who gives, he knows Who takes now.

J.B. stands silent over the parasol.

Mr. Zuss:	Why won't he play the part he's playing?
Nickles:	Because he isn't.
Mr. Zuss:	Isn't what?
Nickles:	Isn't playing. He's not playing. He isn't in the play at all. He's where we all are — in our suffering. Only . . .

Nickles turns savagely on Mr. Zuss.
> . . . Now he knows its Name!

Nickles points dramatically toward the canvas sky. Mr. Zuss's head tilts back following the gesture. He freezes into immobility.

Mr. Zuss:	Look! Look up!
Nickles:	That's your direction.
Mr. Zuss:	Look, I say! The staring stars!
Nickles:	Or only lights not meant . . .

Nickles twists his crooked neck, looks sidewise upward. The canvas sky has disappeared into a profound darkness. There seem to be stars beyond it.

Nickles:	You're mad. You've lost your mind. You're maundering . . .

84

They rise together, their heads back, peering into the darkness overhead.

Nickles: . . . maundering.

Mr. Zuss: Let's get back where we belong.

Nickles: Go on!

Mr. Zuss: No; you.

Nickles: All right . . . together.

They take each other's arm as the light fades.

SCENE SIX

Darkness and silence as before. The drum — a great crash and a long roll fading out. A gray light which has no visible source drifts across the stage where tables and chairs are scattered and overturned. Mr. Zuss and Nickles are huddled together on their platform peering down. J.B., his clothes torn and white with dust, faces what was once the door. The two Messengers, wearing steel helmets and brassards, stand there, carrying Sarah between them.

First Messenger:
She said she lived around here somewhere.
This is all there is.

J.B.: Sarah!

First M.: Where do you want her?

J.B.: Sarah! Sarah!

First M.: On the floor? You got a floor.
You're lucky if you got a floor.

They lay her carefully down. J.B. takes his torn coat off, rolls it into a pillow, kneels to put it under her head.

J.B.: Where was she?

86

First M.: Underneath a wall.
> *indicating Second Messenger*
>> He heard her underneath a wall
>> Calling.
> *to Second Messenger*
>> Tell him what you heard her . . .

Second M.: *imitating*
>> Ruth! . . . Ruth!

First M.: Nobody answered:
>> Nobody could have.

J.B. does not look up or speak. The First Messenger starts toward the door, kicking a fallen chair out of his way.

>> You been down there?
>> Whole block's gone. Bank block. All of it.
>> J.B.'s bank. You know. Just gone.
>> Nothing left to show it ever.
>> Just the hole.

Sarah stirs, opens her eyes. J.B. leans over her. She turns away.

>> J.B.'s millions!
>> That's a laugh now — J.B.'s millions!
>> All he's got is just the hole.
>> Plant went too — all of it — everything.
>> Ask him! Just the hole. He'll tell you.

Sarah: *faintly, her voice following the rhythm of the Second
>> Messenger*
>> Ruth! . . . Ruth!

First M.:   He can tell you.
             He can tell you what he saw.

Sarah: *tonelessly like a voice counting*
             David ... Jonathan ... Mary ... Ruth ...
             I cannot say the last.

J.B.: *his hands on hers*   Rebecca.

Sarah: David ... Jonathan ... Mary ... Ruth ...

J.B.: *looking up over his shoulder, to the Second Messenger*
             You didn't find ... there wasn't ...

First M.:   Tell him.
             Tell him what you heard.

Second M.:   I heard
             Two words. I don't know what they mean.
             I have brought them to you like a pair of pebbles
             Picked up in a path or a pair of
             Beads that might belong to somebody.

J.B.:   There wasn't ... anyone beside?

Second M.: *almost a whisper*
             I only am escaped alone to tell thee.

Sarah: David ... Jonathan ... Mary ... Ruth ...

J.B.:   Sarah!

Silence.

Listen to me!

Silence.

Sarah!
Even desperate we can't despair —
Let go each other's fingers — sink
Numb in that dumb silence — drown there
Sole in our cold selves . . .

We cannot! . . .

God is there too, in the desperation.
I do not know why God should strike
But God is what is stricken also:
Life is what despairs in death
And, desperate, is life still . . .

Sarah!
Do not let my hand go, Sarah!

Say it after me:

The Lord
Giveth . . . Say it.

Sarah: *mechanically*   The Lord giveth.

J.B.:   The Lord taketh away . . .

Sarah: *flinging his hand from hers, shrieking*
Takes!
Kills! Kills! Kills! Kills!

Silence.

J.B.:   Blessed be the name of the Lord.

The light fades.

SCENE SEVEN

Darkness. Silence. Then, out of the dark, Mr. Zuss's voice. It has recovered its confidence and timbre.

Mr. Zuss: Well, my friend . . .

The platform comes into light, Mr. Zuss and Nickles are still where they were, leaning over, elbows on the rail. They straighten up, stretching.

                                    . . . you see the position.
You see how it all comes out in the end.
Your fears were quite unfounded, weren't they?

Nickles: *sourly*
              My fears for you?

Mr. Zuss: For me? . . . For me!
Why should you fear for me?

Nickles: I can't
Think!

Mr. Zuss: No, for him.

Nickles: That ham!

Mr. Zuss: Ham?

91

Nickles: Ham!

Mr. Zuss: *pleasantly*   And you've been telling me
                Over and over that —
                Isn't acting even: only
                Living — breathing . . .

Nickles: Man can muff his
                Life as badly as his lines and louder.
                In it or out of it he's ham.
                He wouldn't understand if twenty
                Thousand suffocating creatures
                Shrieked and tore their tongues out at him
                Choking in a bombed-out town. He'd be
                Thankful!

Mr. Zuss: *stiffly*   I think he understands it
                Perfectly! I think that great
                Yea-saying to the world was wonderful —
                That wounded and deliberate Amen —
                That — affirmation!

Nickles: Affirmation!
                Ever watch the worms affirming?
                Ever hear a hog's Amen
                Just when the knife first hurt? Death is
                Good for you! It makes you glisten!
                Get the large economy container,
                Five for the price of one!

                          You think it's
        Wonderful . . .

He wheels on Mr. Zuss in a sudden fury.

I think it stinks!
One daughter raped and murdered by an idiot,
Another crushed by stones, a son
Destroyed by some fool officer's stupidity,
Two children smeared across a road
At midnight by a drunken child —
And all with God's consent! — foreknowl-
edge! —
And he blesses God!

*Nickles points dramatically at the white, calm, unconcerned
mask in Mr. Zuss's hands.*

It isn't decent!
It isn't moral even! It's disgusting!
His weeping wife in her despair
And he beside her on his trembling ham-bones
Praising God! . . . It's nauseating!

Mr. Zuss: You don't lose gracefully, do you?

Nickles: *snarling*   I don't
             Lose.

Mr. Zuss: You have.

Nickles: That's not the end of it.

Mr. Zuss: No, but that's the *way* it ends.

Nickles: Could have ended.

Mr. Zuss: What do you mean?

Nickles:	Would have, if God had been content
	With this poor crawling victory. He isn't.
	Still He must pursue, still follow —
	Hunt His creature through his branching veins
	With agony until no peace is left him —
	All one blazing day of pain:
	Corner him, compel the answer.
	He cannot rest until He wrings
	The proof of pain, the ultimate certainty.
	God always asks the proof of pain.
Mr. Zuss:	And Job, in his affliction, gives it.
Nickles:	No! God overreaches at the end —
	Pursues too far — follows too fearfully.
	He seals him in his sack of skin
	And scalds his skin to crust to squeeze
	The answer out, but Job evades Him.
Mr. Zuss:	Who can evade the will of God!
	It waits at every door we open.
	What does Dante say? His will . . .
Nickles:	Don't chant that chill equation at me!
Mr. Zuss:	His will: our peace.
Nickles:	Will was never peace, no matter
	Whose will, whose peace.
	Will is rule: surrender is surrender.
	You *make* your peace: you don't give in to it.
	Job will make his own cold peace
	When God pursues him in the web too far —

Implacable, eternal Spider.
A man can always cease: it's something —
A judgment anyway: reject
The whole creation with a stale pink pill.

Mr. Zuss: World is Will. Job can't reject it.

Nickles: God has forgotten what a man can do
Once his body hurts him — once
Pain has penned him in where only
Pain has room to breathe. He learns!
He learns to spit his broken teeth out —
Spit the dirty world out — spit!

Mr. Zuss: And that's the end of everything — to *spit?*

Nickles: Better than that other end
Of pain, of physical agony, of suffering
God prepares for all His creatures.

Mr. Zuss: *Is* it better? *Is* it better?
Job has suffered and praised God.
Would Job be better off asleep
Among the clods of earth in ignorance?

Nickles: Yes, when he suffers in his body:
Yes, when his suffering is *him.*

Mr. Zuss: His suffering will praise.

Nickles: It will not.

Mr. Zuss: Well,
We still have time to see.

Nickles: Put on your
Mask! You'll see!

The light has faded but the faces of the actors are still visible.

Mr. Zuss: *raising his mask*   Put on your own!

Nickles leans over to find it, searching the floor of the platform with his hands. A long silence. From the silence at length:

The Distant Voice:
　　　　　Hast thou considered my servant Job
　　　　　That there is none like him on the earth,
　　　　　A perfect and an upright man, one
　　　　　That feareth God and escheweth evil?

Nickles:　　　Wait a minute! I can't find...

The Distant Voice: *louder*
　　　　　And still he holdeth fast his integrity...

Nickles:　　　Wait a minute, can't you? What the...

The Distant Voice: *almost a whisper*
　　　　　Although thou movedst me against him
　　　　　To destroy him...

Nickles rises, his mask in his two hands. He wheels on Mr. Zuss only to see that Mr. Zuss also has his mask in his hands and stands staring up into the canvas sky.

The Distant Voice is barely audible.

　　　　　　　　without cause...

Silence. The two old actors stand side by side, holding their masks, their heads moving slowly together as they search the dark.

Nickles: Who said that?

Silence.

Mr. Zuss: They want us to go on.

Nickles: Why don't you?

Mr. Zuss: He was asking *you.*

Nickles: Who was?

Mr. Zuss: He was.

Nickles: Prompter probably. Prompter somewhere.
              Your lines he was reading weren't they?

Mr. Zuss: Yes but ...

Nickles: *shouting*   Anybody there?

Silence.

Mr. Zuss: They want us to go on. I told you.

Nickles: Yes. They want us to go on ...
              I don't like it.

Mr. Zuss: We began it.

They put their masks on slowly. The lights fade out. The huge shadows appear on the canvas sky, facing each other.

Godmask: ... And still he holdeth fast his integrity
                Although thou movedst me against him
                To destroy him ...

His voice breaks.

                             without cause.

Satanmask: Skin for skin, yea, all that a man
                Hath will he give for his life.
                But put forth thine hand now and touch
                His bone and his flesh
                And he will curse thee to thy face.

The God-shadow raises its arm again in the formal gesture of contemptuous commitment.

Godmask: Behold he is in thine hand ...

The God-shadow turns away. Silence.

                             but ...
        Save his life!

The two shadows lean together over the earth.

      Note: A second break in the action may be
      made here if it is thought desirable.

SCENE EIGHT

There is no light but the glow on the canvas sky, which holds the looming, leaning shadows. They fade as a match is struck. It flares in Sarah's hand, showing her face, and glimmers out against the wick of a dirty lantern. As the light of the lantern rises, J.B. is seen lying on the broken propped-up table, naked but for a few rags of clothing. Sarah looks at him in the new light, shudders, lets her head drop into her hands. There is a long silence and then a movement in the darkness of the open door where four women and a young girl stand, their arms filled with blankets and newspapers. They come forward slowly into the light.

Nickles: *unseen, his cracked, cackling voice drifting down from the darkness of the platform overhead*

> Never fails! Never fails!
> Count on you to make a mess of it!
> Every blessed blundering time
> You hit at one man you blast thousands.
> Think of that Flood of yours — a massacre!
> Now you've fumbled it again:
> Tumbled a whole city down
> To blister one man's skin with agony.

Nickles' white coat appears at the foot of the ladder. The women, in the circle of the lantern, are walking slowly around J.B. and Sarah, staring at them as though they were figures in a show window.

Nickles: Look at your works! Those shivering women
                  Sheltering under any crumbling
                  Heap to keep the sky out! Weeping!

Mrs. Adams: That's him.

Jolly Adams: Who's him?

Mrs. Adams: Grammar, Jolly.

Mrs. Lesure: Who did she say it was?

Mrs. Murphy: Him she said it was.
                  Poor soul!

Mrs. Lesure: Look at them sores on him!

Mrs. Adams: Don't look, child. You'll remember them.

Jolly Adams: *proudly*
                  Every sore I seen I remember.

Mrs. Botticelli:
                  Who did she say she said it was?

Mrs. Murphy: Him.

Mrs. Adams: That's his wife.

Mrs. Lesure: She's pretty.

Mrs. Botticelli: Ain't she.
                  Looks like somebody we've seen.

Mrs. Adams: *snooting her*
        I don't believe you would have seen her:
        Picture possibly — her picture
        Posed in the penthouse.

Mrs. Botticelli: Puce with pants?

Mrs. Adams: No, the negligee.

Mrs. Botticelli: The net?

Mrs. Adams: The simple silk.

Mrs. Botticelli: Oh la! With sequins?

Mrs. Murphy:
        Here's a place to park your poodle —
        Nice cool floor.

Mrs. Lesure: Shove over, dearie.

The women settle themselves on their newspapers off at the edge of the circle of light. Nickles has perched himself on a chair at the side. Silence.

J.B.: *a whisper*
        God, let me die!

Nickles leers up into the dark toward the unseen platform.

Sarah: *her voice dead*   You think He'd help you
        Even to that?

Silence. Sarah looks up, turning her face away from J.B. She speaks without passion, almost mechanically.

Sarah: God is our enemy

J.B.:   No ... No ... No ... Don't
                       Say that Sarah!

Sarah's head turns toward him slowly as though dragged against her will. She stares and cannot look away.

                              God has something
                       Hidden from our hearts to show.

Nickles: She knows! She's looking at it!

J.B.:   Try to
                       Sleep.

Sarah: *bitterly*   He should have kept it hidden.

J.B.:   Sleep now.

Sarah: You don't have to see it:
                       I do.

J.B.:   Yes, I know.

Nickles: *a cackle*   He knows!
                       He's back behind it and he knows!
                       If he could see what she can see
                       There's something else he might be knowing.

J.B.:   Once I knew a charm for sleeping —

                       Not as forgetfulness but gift,
                       Not as sleep but second sight,

Come and from my eyelids lift
The dead of night.

Sarah: The dead . . .
                                    of night . . .

She drops her head to her knees, whispering.

Come and from my eyelids lift
The dead of night.

Silence.

J.B.:   Out of sleep
Something of our own comes back to us:
A drowned man's garment from the sea.

*Sarah turns the lantern down. Silence. Then the voices of
the women, low.*

Mrs. Botticelli:
        Poor thing!

Mrs. Murphy: Poor thing!
Not a chick nor a child between them.

Mrs. Adams: First their daughters. Then their sons.

Mrs. Murphy: First son first. Blew him to pieces.
More mischance it was than war.
Asleep on their feet in the frost they walked
        into it.

Mrs. Adams: Two at the viaduct: that makes three.

Jolly Adams: *a child's chant*
               Jolly saw the picture! the picture!

Mrs. Adams: Jolly Adams, you keep quiet.

Jolly Adams: Wanna know? The whole of the viaduct . . .

Mrs. Adams: Never again will you look at them! Never!

Mrs. Lesure: Them magazines! They're awful! Which?

Mrs. Murphy: And after that the little one.

Mrs. Botticelli: Who in the
          World are they talking about, the little one?
          What are they talking?

Mrs. Lesure: I don't know.
          Somebody dogged by death it must be.

Mrs. Botticelli:
          Him it must be.

Mrs. Lesure: Who's him?

Mrs. Adams: You know who.

Mrs. Murphy: You remember the . . .

Mrs. Adams: Hush! The child!

Mrs. Murphy: Back of the lumberyard.

Mrs. Lesure: Oh! Him!

Mrs. Murphy: Who did you think it was —
          Penthouse and negligees, daughters and dying?

Mrs. Botticelli:
          Him? That's him? That millionaire?

Mrs. Lesure: Millionaires he buys like cabbages.

Mrs. Murphy: He couldn't buy cabbages now by the look of
          him:
          The rags he's got on.

Mrs. Botticelli: Look at them sores!

Mrs. Murphy: All that's left him now is her.

Mrs. Botticelli:
          Still that's something — a good woman.

Mrs. Murphy: What good is a woman to him with that hide
          on him? —
          Or he to her if you think of it.

Mrs. Adams: Don't!

Mrs. Lesure: Can you blame her?

Mrs. Murphy: I don't blame her.
          All I say is she's no comfort.
          She won't cuddle.

Mrs. Adams: Really, Mrs. . . .

Mrs. Murphy: Murphy call me. What's got into you? . . .
             Nothing recently I'd hazard.

Mrs. Adams: You're not so young yourself, my woman.

Mrs. Murphy: Who's your woman? I was Murphy's.

Mrs. Lesure: None of us are maids entirely.

Mrs. Murphy: Maids in mothballs some might be.

Mrs. Adams: Who might?

Mrs. Murphy: You might.

Mrs. Adams: You! you're . . . historical!

Mrs. Murphy: I never slept a night in history!

Mrs. Botticelli:
             I have. Oh, my mind goes back.

Mrs. Adams: None of that! We have a child here!

Silence.

             How far back?

Mrs. Botticelli: I often wonder.
             Farther than the first but . . . where?

Mrs. Murphy: What do you care? It's lovely country.

Silence.

        Roll a little nearer, dearie,
        Me back side's froze.

Mrs. Lesure: You smell of roses.

Mrs. Murphy: Neither do you but you're warm.

Mrs. Botticelli: Well,
        Good night, ladies. Good night, ladies . . .

Silence. Out of the silence, felt rather than heard at first, a sound of sobbing, a muffled, monotonous sound like the heavy beat of a heart.

J.B.:   If you could only sleep a little
        Now they're quiet, now they're still.

Sarah: *her voice broken*
        I try. But oh I close my eyes and . . .
        Eyes are open there to meet me!

Silence. Then Sarah's voice in an agony of bitterness.

        My poor babies! Oh, my babies!

J.B. pulls himself painfully up, sits huddled on his table in the feeble light of the lamp, his rags about him.

J.B.: *gently*   Go to sleep.

Sarah: Go! Go where?
                     If there were darkness I'd go there.
                     If there were night I'd lay me down in it.
                     God has shut the night against me.
                     God has set the dark alight
                     With horror blazing blind as day
                     When I go toward it . . .
                                             close my eyes.

J.B.:   I know. I know those waking eyes.
                     His will is everywhere against us —
                     Even in our sleep, our dreams . . .

Nickles: *a snort of laughter up toward the dark of the platform*
                     Your will, *his* peace!
                     Doesn't seem to grasp that, does he?
                     Give him another needling twinge
                     Between the withers and the works —
                     He'll understand you better.

J.B.:   If I
                     Knew . . . If I knew why!

Nickles: If he knew
                     Why he wouldn't be there. He'd be
                     Strangling, drowning, suffocating,
                     Diving for a sidewalk somewhere . . .

J.B.:   What I *can't* bear is the blindness —
                     Meaninglessness — the numb blow
                     Fallen in the stumbling night.

Sarah: *starting violently to her feet*
                     Has death no meaning? Pain no meaning?

She points at his body.

>Even these suppurating sores —
>Have they no meaning for you?

Nickles: Ah!

J.B.: *from his heart's pain*
>God will not punish without cause.

Nickles doubles up in a spasm of soundless laughter.

J.B.:   God is just.

Sarah: *hysterically*   God is just!
>If God is just our slaughtered children
>Stank with sin, were rotten with it!

She controls herself with difficulty, turns toward him, reaches her arms out, lets them fall.

>Oh, my dear! my dear! my dear!
>Does God demand deception of us? —
>Purchase His innocence by ours?
>Must we be guilty for Him? — bear
>The burden of the world's malevolence
>For Him who made the world?

J.B.:   *He*
>Knows the guilt is mine. He must know:
>Has He not punished it? He knows its
>Name, its time, its face, its circumstance,
>The figure of its day, the door,
>The opening of the door, the room, the mo-
>   ment . . .

Sarah: *fiercely*

> And you? Do you? You do not know it.
> Your punishment is all you know.

She moves toward the door, stops, turns.

> I will not stay here if you lie —
> Connive in your destruction, cringe to it:
> Not if you betray my children . . .

> I will not stay to listen . . .

> They are
> Dead and they were innocent: I will not
> Let you sacrifice their deaths
> To make injustice justice and God good!

J.B.: *covering his face with his hands*

> My heart beats. I cannot answer it.

Sarah:

> If you buy quiet with their innocence —
> Theirs or yours . . .

softly   I will not love you.

J.B.:

> I have no choice but to be guilty.

Sarah: *her voice rising*

> We have the choice to live or die,
> All of us . . .

> curse God and die . . .

Silence.

J.B.:   God is God or we are nothing —
                  Mayflies that leave their husks behind —
                  Our tiny lives ridiculous — a suffering
                  Not even sad that Someone Somewhere
                  Laughs at as we laugh at apes.
                  We have no choice but to be guilty.
                  God is unthinkable if we are innocent.

Sarah turns, runs soundlessly out of the circle of light, out of the door. The women stir. Mrs. Murphy comes up on her elbow.

Mrs. Murphy: What did I say? I said she'd walk out on him.

Mrs. Lesure: She did.

Mrs. Botticelli: Did she?

Mrs. Murphy: His hide was too much for her.

Mrs. Botticelli:
      His hide or his heart.

Mrs. Murphy: The hide comes between.

Mrs. Botticelli:
      The heart is the stranger.

Mrs. Murphy: Oh, strange!
      It's always strange the heart is: only
      It's the skin we ever know.

J.B.: *raising his head*
　　　　　Sarah, why do you not speak to me? ...
　　　　　Sarah!

Silence.

Mrs. Adams:　　　Now he knows.

Mrs. Murphy:　　　　　　　And he's alone now.

J.B.'s head falls forward onto his knees. Silence. Out of the silence his voice in an agony of prayer.

J.B.:　　　　Show me my guilt, O God!

Nickles:　　　　　　　　*His*
　　　　　Guilt! His! You heard that didn't you?
　　　　　He wants to feel the feel of guilt —
　　　　　That putrid poultice of the soul
　　　　　That draws the poison in, not out —
　　　　　Inverted catheter! You going to show him?

Silence. Nickles rises, moves toward the ladder.

　　　　　Well? You going to show him ... Jahveh?

Silence. He crosses to the ladder's foot.

　　　　　Where are those cold comforters of yours
　　　　　Who justify the ways of God to
　　　　　Job by making Job responsible? —
　　　　　Those three upholders of the world —
　　　　　Defenders of the universe — where are they?

Silence. He starts up the ladder. Stops. The jeering tone is gone. His voice is bitter.

Must be almost time for comfort! . . .

Nickles vanishes into the darkness above. The light fades.

SCENE NINE

Darkness.

J.B.'s Voice: If I had perished from the womb, not having
                Been . . .

*A light without source rises slowly like the light at evening
which enlarges everything. The canvas walls dissolve into distance, the canvas sky into endlessness. The platform has been
pushed away to the side until only the ladder is visible. The
women and the child are huddled together like sleeping figures
on a vast plain. J.B. is alone in an enormous loneliness. Out of
that seeming distance the Three Comforters come shuffling
forward dressed in worn-out clothing. Zophar, a fat, red-faced
man wears the wreck of a clerical collar. Eliphaz, lean and
dark, wears an intern's jacket which once was white. Bildad is
a squat, thick man in a ragged wind-breaker. The women do
not see them, but Jolly Adams sits suddenly up clapping her
hands to her mouth. J.B., his head on his arms, sees nothing.*

J.B.:   Death cannot heal me . . .
                                              Death
                Will leave my having been behind it
                Like a bear's foot festering in a trap . . .

Jolly Adams: *her voice rising word by word to a scream*
                Look! Look! Look! Look!
                Mother! Mother!

*The women pull themselves up. The Three Comforters shuffle
on, squat in the rubbish around J.B.: Zophar lighting the stub
of a fat, ragged cigar; Eliphaz lighting a broken pipe; Bildad
lighting a crumpled cigarette.*

Mrs. Murphy: Agh, the scavengers!

Mrs. Botticelli:
          Three old pokey crows they look like.

Mrs. Murphy:
          They are, too. It's the smell of the suffering.
          See that leather-backed old bucket? —
          Kind of character you hear from
          Sundays in a public park
          Pounding the hell out of everything . . . *you*
             know.

Mrs. Botticelli:
          I know. Wall Street. Bakers. Bankers.

Mrs. Lesure: All the answers in a book.

Mrs. Botticelli:
          Russkys got them all — the answers.

Mrs. Murphy:
          Characters like that, they smell the
          Human smell of heartsick misery
          Farther than a kite smells carrion.

Mrs. Lesure: Who's the collar?

Mrs. Murphy: Some spoiled priest.

Mrs. Botticelli:
          They can smell it farther even.

Mrs. Lesure: Not as far as dead-beat doctors:
          They're the nosies.

Mrs. Murphy: Let them nose!
          a tremendous yawn
          Ohhh, I'm halfway over . . .
                                        drownding
          Down and down . . .
                              I hear the seagulls
          Singing soundings in the sea . . .

*She lets herself fall back on her newspapers. The others follow
one by one.*

Jolly Adams: I don't hear them.

Mrs. Botticelli: Pound your ears.

Mrs. Lesure: Slip your moorings . . . Oh, I'm numb.

Mrs. Murphy: Come alongside, dear.

Mrs. Lesure: I'm coming.

Mrs. Botticelli:
          That doctor one, he makes me creep.

Mrs. Murphy: Keep your thumb on your thoughts or he'll
diddle them.

Mrs. Botticelli:
Let him pry: he'll lose an eyeball.

Mrs. Lesure: He's a peeper. Watch your sleep.

Mrs. Murphy: Who was she, all gore, all story,
Dabbled in a deep blood sea,
And what she washed in, that was she?

Mrs. Lesure: *from her dream*
Some queen of Scotland...

Mrs. Murphy: Queen of Scones...

*A long silence. The Three Comforters squat smoking and
waiting. At length J.B. pulls himself painfully up to kneel on
his table, his face raised.*

J.B.: *a whisper*
God! My God! My God! What have I
Done?

Silence.

Bildad: *removing his cigarette*
Fair question, Big Boy.
Anyone answer you yet? No answer?

Zophar: *removing his cigar*
That was answered long ago —
Long ago.

Eliphaz: *knocking out his pipe*
                         In dreams are answers.
                  How do your dreams go, Big Boy? Tell!

J.B.: *peering*
                  Is someone there? Where? I cannot
                  See you in this little light
                  My eyes too fail me . . .

Silence.

                                            Who is there?

Silence.

                  I know how ludicrous I must look,
                  Covered with rags, my skin pustulent . . .

Silence.

                  I know . . .

Silence.

                                   I know how others see me.

A long silence.

                  Why have you come?

Bildad: *a coarse laugh*   For comfort, Big Boy.
                  Didn't you ring?

Zophar: *a fat laugh*   That's it: for comfort!

Eliphaz: *a thin laugh*
          All the comfort you can find.

Bildad: All the kinds of.

Eliphaz: *All* the comforts.

Zophar: You called us and we came.

J.B.:   I called
          God.

Bildad: Didn't you!

Eliphaz: Didn't you just!

Zophar: Why should God reply to *you*
          From the blue depths of His Eternity?

Eliphaz: Blind depths of His Unconsciousness?

Bildad: Blank depths of His Necessity?

Zophar: God is far above in Mystery.

Eliphaz: God is far below in Mindlessness.

Bildad: God is far within in History —
          Why should God have time for you?

J.B.:   The hand of God has touched me. Look at me!
          Every hope I ever had,
          Every task I put my mind to,
          Every work I've ever done

Annulled as though I had not done it.
My trace extinguished in the land,
My children dead, my father's name
Obliterated in the sunlight everywhere ...

Love too has left me.

Bildad: Love!
    a great guffaw
            What's love to Him? One man's misery!

J.B.: *hardly daring*
            If I am innocent ...?

Bildad: *snort of jeering laughter*   Innocent! Innocent!
            Nations shall perish in their innocence.
            Classes shall perish in their innocence.
            Young men in slaughtered cities
            Offering their silly throats
            Against the tanks in innocence shall perish.
            What's your innocence to theirs?
            God is History. If you offend Him
            Will not History dispense with you?
            History has no time for innocence.

J.B.:   God is just. We are not squeezed
            Naked through a ridiculous orifice
            Like bulls into a blazing ring
            To blunder there by blindfold laws
            We never learn or can, deceived by
            Stratagems and fooled by feints,
            For sport, for nothing, till we fall
            We're pricked so badly.

Bildad: *all park-bench orator*   Screw your justice!
                History is justice! — time
                Inexorably turned to truth! —
                Not for one man. For humanity.
                One man's life won't measure on it.
                One man's suffering won't count, no matter
                What his suffering; but All will.
                At the end there will be justice! —
                Justice for All! Justice for everyone!
        subsiding
                On the way — it doesn't matter.

J.B.:   Guilt matters. Guilt must always matter.
                Unless guilt matters the whole world is
                Meaningless. God too is nothing.

Bildad: *losing interest*
                You may be guiltier than Hell
                As History counts guilt and not
                One smudging thumbprint on your conscience.
                Guilt is a sociological accident:
                Wrong class — wrong century —
                You pay for your luck with your licks, that's all.

*Eliphaz has been fidgeting. Now he breaks in like a professor
in a seminar, poking a forefinger at the air.*

Eliphaz: Come! Come! Come! Guilt is a
                Psychophenomenal situation —
                An illusion, a disease, a sickness:
                That filthy feeling at the fingers,
                Scent of dung beneath the nails ...

Zophar: *outraged, flushed, head thrown back*
>   Guilt is illusion? Guilt is reality! —
>   The one reality there is!
>   All mankind are guilty always!

Bildad: *jeering*
>   The Fall of Man it felled us all!

J.B.'s voice breaks through the squabbling with something of its old authority.

J.B.:
>   No doubt ye are the people
>   And wisdom shall die with you! I am
>   Bereaved, in pain, desperate, and you mock me!
>   There was a time when men found pity
>   Finding each other in the night:
>   Misery to walk with misery —
>   Brother in whose brother-guilt
>   Guilt could be conceived and recognized.
>   We have forgotten pity.

Eliphaz: No.
>   We have surmounted guilt. It's quite,
>   Quite different, isn't it? You see the difference.
>   Science knows now that the sentient spirit
>   Floats like the chambered nautilus on a sea
>   That drifts it under skies that drive:
>   Beneath, the sea of the subconscious;
>   Above, the winds that wind the world.
>   Caught between that sky, that sea,
>   Self has no will, cannot be guilty.
>   The sea drifts. The sky drives.
>   The tiny, shining bladder of the soul

Washes with wind and wave or shudders
Shattered between them.

Zophar: Blasphemy!

Bildad: Bullshit!

Eliphaz: *oblivious*
           There is no guilt, my man. We all are
           Victims of our guilt, not guilty.
           We kill the king in ignorance: the voice
           Reveals: we blind ourselves. At our
           Beginning, in the inmost room,
           Each one of us, disgusting monster
           Changed by the chilling moon to child,
           Violates his mother. Are we guilty?
           Our guilt is underneath the Sybil's
           Stone: not known.

J.B.: *violently*   I'd rather suffer
           Every unspeakable suffering God sends,
           Knowing it was I that suffered,
           I that earned the need to suffer,
           I that acted, I that chose,
           Than wash my hands with yours in that
           Defiling innocence. Can we be men
           And make an irresponsible ignorance
           Responsible for everything? I will not
           Listen to you!

J.B. pulls his rags over his head.

Eliphaz: *shrugging*   But you will. You will.

123

Zophar: Ah, my son, how well you said that!
                        How well you said it! Without guilt
                        What is a man? An animal, isn't he?
                        A wolf forgiven at his meat,
                        A beetle innocent in his copulation.
                        What divides us from the universe
                        Of blood and seed, conceives the soul in us,
                        Brings us to God, but guilt? The lion
                        Dies of death: we die of suffering.
                        The lion vanishes: our souls accept
                        Eternities of reparation.
                        But for our guilt we too would vanish,
                        Bundles of corrupting bones
                        Bagged in a hairless hide and rotting.
                        Happy the man whom God correcteth!
                        He tastes his guilt. His hope begins.
                        He is in league with the stones in certainty.

*J.B. pulls his rags from his head, drags himself around toward
the voice.*

J.B.:   Teach me and I will hold my tongue.
                        Show me my transgression.

Zophar: *gently*   No.
                        No, my son. You show *me*.

He hunches forward dropping his voice.

                        Search your inmost heart! Question it!
                        Guilt is a deceptive secret,
                        The labor often of years, a work

Conceived in infancy, brought to birth
In unpredictable forms years after:
At twelve the palpable elder brother;
At seventeen, perhaps, the servant
Seen by the lamp by accident...

J.B.: *urgently, the words forced from him*   My
Sin! Teach me my sin! My wickedness!
Surely iniquity that suffers
Judgment like mine cannot be secret.
Mine is no childish fault, no nastiness
Concealed behind a bathroom door,
No sin a prurient virtue practices
Licking the silence from its lips
Like sugar afterwards. Mine is flagrant,
Worthy of death, of many deaths,
Of shame, loss, hurt, indignities
Such as these! Such as these!
Speak of the sin I must have sinned
To suffer what you see me suffer.

Zophar: Do we need to name our sins
To know the need to be forgiven?
Repent, my son! Repent!

J.B.: *an agony of earnestness*   I sit here
Such as you see me. In my soul
I suffer what you guess I suffer.
Tell me the wickedness that justifies it.
Shall I repent of sins I have not
Sinned to understand it? Till I
Die I will not violate my integrity.

125

Zophar: *a fat chuckle*
>Your integrity! Your integrity!
>What integrity have you? —
>A man, a miserable, mortal, sinful,
>Venal man like any other.
>You squat there challenging the universe
>To tell you what your crime is called,
>Thinking, because your life was virtuous,
>It can't be called. It can. Your sin is
>Simple. You were born a man!

J.B.:
>What is my fault? What have I done?

Zophar: *thundering*
>What is your fault? Man's heart is evil!
>What have you done? Man's will is evil.
>Your fault, your sin, are heart and will:
>The worm at heart, the wilful will
>Corrupted with its foul imagining.

J.B. crouches lower in his rags. Silence.

J.B.:
>Yours is the cruelest comfort of them all,
>Making the Creator of the Universe
>The miscreator of mankind —
>A party to the crimes He punishes . . .
>
>Making my sin . . .
>>a horror . . .
>>>a deformity . . .

Zophar: *collapsing into his own voice*
>If it were otherwise we could not bear it . . .

Without the fault, without the Fall,
We're madmen: all of us are madmen ...

He sits staring at his hands, then repeats the phrase:

Without the Fall
We're madmen all.
We watch the stars
That creep and crawl ...

Bildad: Like dying flies
Across the wall
Of night ...

Eliphaz: and shriek ...
And that is all.

Zophar: Without the Fall ...

A long silence. Out of the silence at last J.B.'s voice, barely audible.

J.B.:   God, my God, my God, answer me!*

Silence.

His voice rises.

I cry out of wrong but I am not heard ...
I cry aloud but there is no judgment.

Silence.

violently

Though He slay me, yet will I trust in Him ...

Silence.

His voice drops.

But I will maintain my own ways before Him . . .

Silence.

The ancient human cry.

Oh, that I knew where I might find Him! —
That I might come even to His seat!
I would order my cause before Him
And fill my mouth with arguments.

There is a rushing sound in the air.

Behold,
I go forward but He is not there,
Backward, but I cannot perceive Him . . .

*Out of the rushing sound, the Distant Voice; J.B. cowers as he
hears it, his rags over his head.*

The Distant Voice:
Who is this that darkeneth counsel
By words without knowledge? . . .

Where wast thou
When I laid the foundations of the earth . . .

When the morning stars sang together
And all the sons of God shouted for
Joy?

Hast *thou* commanded the morning?

Hast *thou* entered into the springs of the sea
Or hast *thou* walked in the search of the depth?

Have the gates of death been opened unto *thee?*

Where is the way where light dwelleth?
And as for darkness, where is the place thereof?

Hast thou entered into the treasures of the snow?

By what way is the light parted
Which scattereth the east wind upon the earth?

Can'st thou bind the sweet influences of the
    Pleiades?

Hast thou given the horse strength?
Hast thou clothed his neck with thunder?

He saith among the trumpets, Ha, ha;
He smelleth the battle afar off,
The thunder of the captains and the shouting.

Doth the eagle mount up at thy command?

Her eyes behold afar off.
Her young ones also suck up blood:
And where the slain are, there is she...

*The rushing sound dies away. The Three Comforters stir un-
easily, peering up into the darkness. One by one they rise.*

129

Bildad: The wind's gone round.

Zophar: It's cold.

Bildad: I told you.

Eliphaz: I hear the silence like a sound.

Zophar: Wait for me!

Bildad: The wind's gone round.

They go out as they came. Silence. J.B. sits motionless, his head covered. The rushing sound returns like the second, stronger gust of a great storm. The Voice rises above it.

The Distant Voice:
                 Shall he that contendeth with the Almighty
                        instruct
                 Him? . . .

The rushing sound dies away again. The women sit up, huddle together.

Jolly Adams: *screaming*
                        Mother! Mother! what was
                 That?

Mrs. Adams: The wind, child. Only the wind.
                 Only the wind.

Jolly Adams: I heard a word.

Mrs. Adams: You heard the thunder in the wind.

Jolly Adams: *drowsy*
>Under the wind there was a word...

Mrs. Adams picks her up. The women gather their newspapers and blankets and stumble out into the darkness through the door. For the third time the rushing sound returns.

The Distant Voice:
>He that reproveth God, let him answer it!

J.B.:
>Behold, I am vile; what shall I answer thee?
>I will lay mine hand upon my mouth.

The Distant Voice:
>Gird up thy loins like a man:
>I will demand of thee, and declare thou unto me.

J.B. pulls himself painfully to his knees.

>Wilt thou disannul my judgment?

J.B. does not answer.

>Wilt thou condemn
>Me that thou mayest be righteous?

>Hast thou an arm like God? Or canst thou
>Thunder with a voice like Him?

>Deck thyself now with majesty and excellency
>And array thyself with glory and beauty...

>Then will I also confess unto thee
>That thine own right hand can save thee.

J.B. raises his bowed head.

J.B.: gently   I know that thou canst do everything . . .

The rushing sound dies away.

>And that no thought can be withholden from thee.
>Who is he that hideth counsel without knowledge?
>Therefore have I uttered that I understood not:
>Things too wonderful for me, which I knew not.
>
>Hear, I beseech thee, and I will speak: . . .

Silence.

>I have heard of thee by the hearing of the ear . . .
>But now . . .

His face is drawn in agony.

>   mine eye seeth thee!

He bows his head. His hands wring each other.

>   Wherefore
>I abhor myself . . . and repent . . .

The light fades.

SCENE TEN

The Platform. As the lights come on the two actors turn vio-
lently away from each other, tearing their masks off. Nickles,
with a gesture of disgust, skims his into a corner.

Nickles: Well, that's that!

Mr. Zuss: That's . . . that!

Silence. After a time Nickles looks cautiously around at Mr.
Zuss.

Nickles: What's the matter with you?

Mr. Zuss: Nothing.

Nickles: You don't look pleased.

Mr. Zuss: Should I?

Nickles: Well,
        You were right weren't you?

Mr. Zuss: *too loud*   Of course I was right.

Nickles: *too soft*
        Anyway, you were magnificent.

Mr. Zuss: Thank you.

He looks at the mask in his hands: puts it down as though it had stung him. Silence. Mr. Zuss pretends to be busy with a shoelace.

Mr. Zuss: Why did you say that?

Nickles: What did I say?

Mr. Zuss: Why did you say it like that?

Nickles: Like what?

Mr. Zuss: *imitating*
              "Anyway!" . . .
                         "*Anyway*, you were magnificent!"

Nickles: You know. "Anyway." Regardless.

Mr. Zuss: Regardless of
              What?

Nickles: Now, wait a minute! Wait a
              Minute! You were magnificent. I said so.

Mr. Zuss: Go on. Finish it.

Nickles: Finish what?

Mr. Zuss: Regardless of . . . ?

Nickles: . . . being right, of course.

What's got into you, my friend? What's eat-
    ing you?
Being magnificent and being right
Don't go together in this universe.
It's being wrong — a desperate stubbornness
Fighting the inextinguishable stars —
Excites imagination. You were
Right. And knew it. And were admirable.
Notwithstanding!
    snickering   anyway!
    a snarl   regardless!

Mr. Zuss: I knew you noticed.

Nickles: Of course I noticed.
            What lover of the art could fail to!

Something in Mr. Zuss's expression stops him.

                                  Noticed
            What?

Mr. Zuss: That tone! That look he gave me!

Nickles: He misconceived the part entirely.

Mr. Zuss: Misconceived the world! Buggered it!

Nickles: Giving in like that! Whimpering!

Mr. Zuss: Giving in! You call that arrogant,
            Smiling, supercilious humility
            Giving in to God?

Nickles: Arrogant!
           His suppurating flesh — his children —
           Let's not talk about those children —
           Everything he ever had!
           And all he asks is answers of the universe:
           All he asks is reasons why —
           Why? Why? And God replies to him:
           God comes whirling in the wind replying —
           What? That God knows more than he does.
           That God's more powerful than he! —
           Throwing the whole creation at him!
           Throwing the Glory and the Power!
           What's the Power to a broken man
           Trampled beneath it like a toad already?
           What's the Glory to a skin that stinks!
           And this ham actor! — what does *he* do?
           How does he play Job to that?
      attitude
           "Thank you!" "I'm a worm!" "Take two!"

           Plays the way a sheep would play it —
           Pious, contemptible, goddam sheep
           Without the spunk to spit on Christmas!

*Mr. Zuss has watched Nickles' mounting rage in silence, star-
ing at him. Nickles breaks off, shuffles, looks at Mr. Zuss, crosses
to the ladder, swings a leg across the rail.*

           Well...

He swings the other over.

           you said he would...

He starts down.

> You're right.

Another rung.

> I'm wrong.

Another.

> You win.

Another.

> God always wins.

He peers down into the dark under the platform.

> Where did I put that ... popcorn?

Mr. Zuss:
> Win!
> Planets and Pleiades and eagles —
> Screaming horses — scales of light —
> The wonder and the mystery of the universe —
> The unimaginable might of things —
> Immeasurable knowledge in the waters some-
> where
> Wandering their ways — the searchless power
> Burning on the hearth of stars —
> Beauty beyond the feel of fingers —
> Marvel beyond the maze of mind —
> The whole creation! And God showed him!

God stood stooping there to show him!
Last Orion! Least sea shell! ...
And what did Job do?

Mr. Zuss has worked himself up into a dramatic fury equaling Nickles'.

Job ... just ... sat!

Silence.

Sat there!

Silence.

Dumb!

Silence.

Until it ended!
Then! ... you heard him!

Mr. Zuss chokes.

Then, he *calmed* me!
Gentled me the way a farmhand
Gentles a bulging, bugling bull!
Forgave me! ...
for the world! ...

for everything!

Nickles: *poking around in the shadow under the platform*
  Nonsense! He repented, didn't he —
  The perfect and the upright man!
  He repented!

Mr. Zuss: That's just it!
  He repented. It was *him* —
  Not the fear of God but *him*!

Nickles: Fear? Of course he feared. Why wouldn't he?
  God with all those stars and stallions!
  He with little children's bones!

Mr. Zuss: *pursuing his mounting indignation*
  ...As though Job's suffering were justified
  Not by the Will of God but Job's
  Acceptance of God's Will ...

Nickles: Well,
  What did you hope for? Hallelujahs?

Mr. Zuss: *not hearing*
  ...In spite of everything he'd suffered!
  In spite of all he'd lost and loved
  He understood and he forgave it! ...

Nickles: *a contemptuous snort as he straightens to face Mr.
  Zuss on the platform*
  What other victory could God win?
  The choice is swallowing this swill of world
  Or vomiting in the trough. Job swallowed it,
  That's your triumph! — that he swallowed it.

Mr. Zuss: ...He'd heard of God and now he saw Him!
               Who's the judge in judgment there?
               Who plays the hero, God or him?
               Is God to be *forgiven?*

Nickles: Isn't he?
               Job was innocent, you may remember...

Silence.

               a nasty singsong
               The perfect and the upright man!

Mr. Zuss: *deflated*
               Don't start that again! I'm sick of it.

Nickles: *You* are!

Mr. Zuss: *I* am. Sick to death.
               *swinging his leg over the rail and starting down the
               ladder*
               I'd rather sell balloons to children...
               Lights!...

He shouts.

                       Turn those lights on, can't you?
               Want to see me break my neck?

The platform lights go out. Total darkness.

Louder.   Lights! Lights! That's not the end of it.

Nickles: *in the darkness*
               Why isn't that the end? It's over.

140

Job has chosen how to choose.
You've made your bow? You want another?

*The dangling light bulbs come feebly on. By their light J.B.
can still be seen kneeling on his broken table. Mr. Zuss and
Nickles crawl under the platform after their traps. Their voices
come from the shadow, punctuated by grunts and wheezes.*

Mr. Zuss: You know as well as I there's more...

There's always one more scene no matter
Who plays Job or how he plays it...

God restores him at the end.

Nickles: *a snort*
God restores us all. That's normal.
That's God's mercy to mankind...

We never asked Him to be born...

We never chose the lives we die of...

They beat our rumps to make us breathe...

But God, if we have suffered patiently,
Borne it in silence, stood the stench,
Rewards us...

gives our dirty selves back.

Mr. Zuss emerges in his white jacket, adjusting his cap.

Mr. Zuss: Souls back!

Nickles: Selves back! Dirty selves
                    We've known too well and never wanted.

Mr. Zuss: That's not this play.

Nickles backs out with his jacket and cap and tray; puts them on.

Nickles: Hell it isn't.

Mr. Zuss tightens his balloon belt.

Mr. Zuss: God restores him *here*. On earth.

Nickles: *balancing his tray*
                    So Job gets his in cash. That's generous.
                    What percentage off for cash?

Mr. Zuss: Gets all he ever had and more —
                    Much more.

Nickles: *cheerfully ironic*
                                        Sure. His wife. His children!

Mr. Zuss: *embarrassed*
                    He gets his wife back, and the children . . .
                    Follow in nature's course.

Nickles, who has stooped to pick up a bag of popcorn, straightens slowly, stares at Mr. Zuss.

142

Nickles: *harshly*   You're lying.

Mr. Zuss: I'm not lying.

Nickles: I say you're lying.

Mr. Zuss: Why should I lie. It's in the Book.

Nickles: *jeering*
          Wife back! Balls! He wouldn't touch her.
          He wouldn't take her with a glove!
          After all that filth and blood and
          Fury to begin again! . . .
          This fetid earth! That frightened Heaven
          Terrified to trust the soul
          It made with Its own hands, but testing it,
          Tasting it, by trial, by torture,
          Over and over till the last, least town
          On all this reeling, reeking earth
          Stinks with a spiritual agony
          That stains the stones with excrement and
            shows
          In shadow on each greasy curtain!
          After life like his to take
          The seed up of the sad creation
          Planting the hopeful world again —
          He can't! . . . he won't! . . . he wouldn't touch
            her!

Mr. Zuss: He does though.

Nickles: *raging*   Live his life again? —
        Not even the most ignorant, obstinate,

Stupid or degraded man
This filthy planet ever farrowed,
Offered the opportunity to live
His bodily life twice over, would accept it —
Least of all Job, poor, trampled bastard!

*Mr. Zuss has finished fooling with his balloons. He straightens
up and marches off without a glance at Nickles.*

It can't be borne twice over! Can't be!

Mr. Zuss: It is though. Time and again it is —
                 Every blessed generation . . .

His voice drifts back as he disappears.

Time and again . . .

Time and again . . .

*Nickles starts to follow, looks back, sees J.B. kneeling in his
rubble, hesitates, crosses, squats behind him, his vendor's cap
pushed back on his head, his tray on his knees.*

Nickles: J.B.!

J.B.:   Let me alone.

Nickles: It's me.

J.B. shrugs.

I'm not the Father. I'm the — Friend.

144

J.B.:   I have no friend.

Nickles: Oh come off it.
                    You don't have to act with me.

J.B. is silent.

                    O.K. Carry on.
                    All I wanted was to help.
                    Professional counsel you might call it ...

J.B. is silent.

                         Of course you know how all this ends? ...

J.B. is silent.

                    I wondered how you'd play the end.

J.B.:   Who knows what the end is, ever?

Nickles: I do. You do.

J.B.:   Then don't tell me.

Nickles: What's the worst thing you can think of?

J.B.:   I have asked for death. Begged for it. Prayed
                    for it.

Nickles: Then the worst thing can't be death.

J.B.:   Ah!

Nickles: You know now.

J.B.:   No. You tell me.

Nickles: Why should I tell you when you know?

J.B.:   Then don't. I'm sick of mysteries. Sick of
         them.

Nickles: He gives it back to you.

J.B.:   What back?

Nickles: All of it.
         Everything He ever took:
         Wife, health, children, everything.

J.B.:   I have no wife.

Nickles: She comes back to you.

J.B.:   I have no children.

Nickles: *a nasty laugh*   You'll have better ones.

J.B.:   My skin is . . .

He breaks off, staring at the skin of his naked arms.

Nickles: Oh come on! I know the
         Look of grease paint!

J.B.:   . . . whole! It's healed!

146

Nickles: *heavily ironic*
> You see? You see what I mean? What He plans
> for you?

J.B., *staring at his arms, is silent.*

Nickles: *leaning forward, urgently*
> Tell me how you play the end.
> Any man was screwed as Job was! . . .

J.B. *does not answer.*

> I'll tell you how you play it. Listen!
> Think of all the mucked-up millions
> Since this buggered world began
> Said, No!, said, Thank you!, took a rope's end,
> Took a window for a door,
> Swallowed something, gagged on something . . .

J.B. *lifts his head: he is listening but not to Nickles.*

> None of them knew the truth as Job does.
> None of them had his cause to know.

J.B.:   Listen! Do you hear? There's someone . . .

Nickles: *violently*
> Job won't take it! Job won't touch it!
> Job will fling it in God's face
> With half his guts to make it spatter!
> He'd rather suffocate in dung —
> Choke in ordure —

J.B.: *rising*   There is someone —
                    Someone waiting at the door.

Nickles: *pulling his cap down, rising slowly*
                                                I know.

The dangling lights dim out.

SCENE ELEVEN

A light comes from the canvas door. It increases as though day were beginning somewhere. Nickles has gone.

J.B.:   Who is it?

He crosses toward the door walking with his old ease. Stops.

                    Is there someone there?

There is no answer. He goes on. Reaches the door.

              Sarah!

The light increases. She is sitting on the sill, a broken twig in her hand.

Sarah: Look, Job: the forsythia,
              The first few leaves ...

                              not leaves though ...

                              petals ...

J.B.: *roughly* Get up!

Sarah: Where shall I go?

J.B.:   Where you went!
                 Wherever!

She does not answer.

More gently.   Where?

Sarah: Among the ashes.
                All there is now of the town is ashes.
                Mountains of ashes. Shattered glass.
                Glittering cliffs of glass all shattered
                Steeper than a cat could climb
                If there were cats still . . .
                                    And the pigeons —
                They wheel and settle and whirl off
                Wheeling and almost settling . . .
                                    And the silence —
                There is no sound there now — no wind
                    sound —
                Nothing that could sound the wind —
                Could make it sing — no door — no door-
                    way . . .

                Only this.

She looks at the twig in her hands.

                        Among the ashes!
                I found it growing in the ashes,
                Gold as though it did not know . . .

Her voice rises hysterically.

I broke the branch to strip the leaves off —
Petals again! . . .

She cradles it in her arms.

But they so clung to it!

J.B.:   Curse God and die, you said to me.

Sarah: Yes.

She looks up at him for the first time, then down again.

You wanted justice, didn't you?
There isn't any. There's the world . . .

She begins to rock on the doorsill, the little branch in her arms.

Cry for justice and the stars
Will stare until your eyes sting. Weep,
Enormous winds will thrash the water.
Cry in sleep for your lost children,
Snow will fall . . .
                    snow will fall . . .

J.B.:   Why did you leave me alone?

Sarah: I loved you.
I couldn't help you any more.
You wanted justice and there was none —
Only love.

J.B.:   He does not love. He
            Is.

Sarah: But we do. That's the wonder.

J.B.:   Yet you left me.

Sarah: Yes, I left you.
            I thought there was a way away...

            Water under bridges opens
            Closing and the companion stars
            Still float there afterwards. I thought the door
            Opened into closing water.

J.B.:   Sarah!

He drops on his knees beside her in the doorway, his arms around her.

Sarah: Oh, I never could!
            I never could! Even the forsythia...

She is half laughing, half crying.

            Even the forsythia beside the
            Stair could stop me.

They cling to each other. Then she rises, drawing him up, peering at the darkness inside the door.

J.B.:   It's too dark to see.

She turns, pulls his head down between her hands and kisses him.

Sarah: Then blow on the coal of the heart, my
                      darling.

J.B.:   The coal of the heart . . .

Sarah: It's all the light now.

Sarah comes forward into the dim room, J.B. behind her. She lifts a fallen chair, sets it straight.

> Blow on the coal of the heart.
> The candles in churches are out.
> The lights have gone out in the sky.
> Blow on the coal of the heart
> And we'll see by and by . . .

J.B. has joined her, lifting and straightening the chairs.

> We'll see where we are.
> The wit won't burn and the wet soul smoulders.
> Blow on the coal of the heart and we'll know . . .
> We'll know . . .

The light increases, plain white daylight from the door, as they work.

CURTAIN